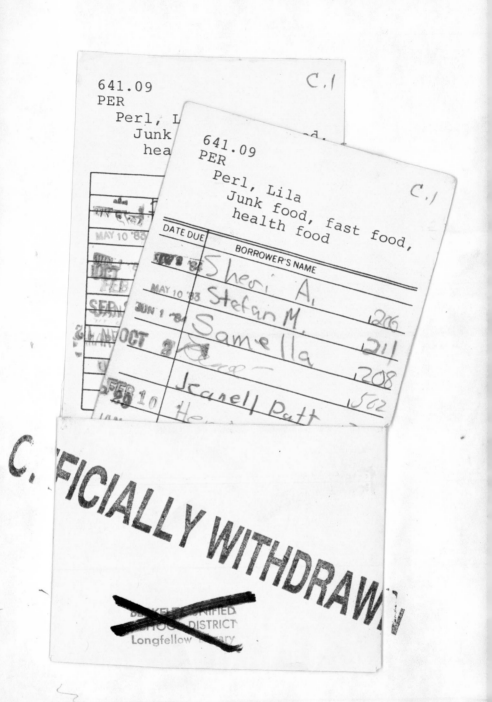

641.09
PER

Perl, L
Junk
hea

641.09
PER

Perl, Lila
Junk food, fast food,
health food

C.1

C.1

DATE DUE	BORROWER'S NAME	
MAY 8 '83	Sheri A.	
MAY 10 '83	Stefan M.	206
JUN 1 '84	Sam·ella	211
OCT 2		208
FEB 20 10	Jeanell Patt	502

MAY 10 '83

JUNK FOOD,
FAST FOOD,
HEALTH FOOD

OTHER FOOD BOOKS BY LILA PERL

SLUMPS, GRUNTS, AND SNICKERDOODLES
What Colonial America Ate and Why

HUNTER'S STEW AND HANGTOWN FRY
What Pioneer America Ate and Why

THE HAMBURGER BOOK
All about Hamburgers and
Hamburger Cookery

JUNK FOOD, FAST FOOD, HEALTH FOOD

WHAT AMERICA EATS AND WHY

by Lila Perl

 Houghton Mifflin/Clarion Books/New York

C.1

Houghton Mifflin/Clarion Books
52 Vanderbilt Avenue, New York, NY 10017

Copyright © 1980 by Lila Perl

Library of Congress Cataloging in Publication Data

Perl, Lila.
Junk food, fast food, health food.
Bibliography: p. 180. Includes index.
Summary: Explores 20th-century American eating
patterns and includes a selection of recipes reflecting
contemporary tastes.
1. Food habits—United States—History—Juvenile
literature.   2. Food, Junk—Juvenile literature.
3. Cookery (Natural foods)—Juvenile literature.
[1. Food habits.   2. Food, Junk.   3. Cookery—
Natural foods]   I. Title.
TX357.P47   641'.0973   80-15928   ISBN 0-395-29108-9

CONTENTS

RECIPE CONTENTS

INTRODUCTION

Not so long ago, nobody in America had ever heard of junk food. Of course, that doesn't mean that there wasn't any. There has probably been junk food in the world ever since the first crude machinery was devised for crushing sugar-cane stalks to extract their juice; ever since millers began trying to grind wheat into the whitest possible flour—discarding the nourishing bran and germ of the grain. So the makings of junk food may reach back almost to the dawn of farming, possibly 7,000 years.

What is "junk food" and why is there so much of it around nowadays that the name for it has sprung up out of our popular culture? "Empty calories" or "high in calories, low in food value" is the way nutritionists describe most of the greasy, breaded, fried, salty, spicy, or heavily sweetened, chemically treated, and additive-laden foods that we eat today: the hot dogs, french fries, doughnuts, frozen desserts, thick shakes, and soft drinks that the fast food chains, especially, dangle before our appetites.

Fast food, as big business, is a phenomenon of twentieth-century America that began to zoom during the 1950s. The hamburgers, fried chicken, and other specialties that today's quick-service restaurants and take-out shops offer their fast-feeding customers cannot *all* be classified as junk food. But many of them can.

Exactly how did junk food and fast food develop and why have they become so popular? To find the answers we'll have to glance back to the century preceding our own, when science and commerce joined forces and got to work on the processing and distribution of the nation's food. In that same era, Americans began moving from farms to cities, and family life in the United States started to undergo some fairly drastic changes. The development of modern convenience foods went hand-in-hand with those changes, helping to revolutionize the American life-style.

Another type of food we hear a great deal about nowadays is health food. The idea of eating a diet of especially nourishing foods is both new and not new in the United States. Starting way back during the first half of the nineteenth century, some people felt that Americans were overeating, indulging in too many fatty meats, too many pies and rich desserts, too many starches, and too much bread made with refined white flour. The followers of a New Jersey minister named Sylvester Graham took up a vegetarian diet of breads and cereals made with whole wheat flour, plenty of fresh fruits and vegetables, and milk. But such health food fans were clearly in the minority in the nineteenth-century United States. Some people regarded them as faddists, even fanatics; others thought of them as the lunatic fringe of American eaters.

The revival of interest in health foods that has taken place since the 1960s probably began as a kind of counterattack by the counterculture. Many young people who "dropped out" of American society to express their dissatisfaction with its military-industrial character also opposed its big-business food products that appeared on supermarket shelves. Some of these young people got together and formed rural communes. There they began to grow and raise their own food "naturally" or organically—without the use of synthetic fertilizers, pesticides, fungicides, or growth hormones. Others espoused vegetarian diets like the strictly disciplined macrobiotic diet that was based on whole grains, or they became devotees of raw foods, or of yogurt and honey, wheat germ and alfalfa sprouts, or natural vitamin therapy. American society, with tolerant amusement, dubbed this group "the granola generation."

Today the junk food camp and the health food camp aren't nearly so far apart as one might imagine. For one thing, the big food companies were quick to jump on the bandwagon in response to the growing interest in health food. By the early 1970s you could buy crunchy, munchy, ready-to-eat granola-type cereals with bits of dried fruit in them right off the supermarket shelf. Only inches away sat the boxes of sugar-coated corn, rice, and other refined-flour breakfast cereals manufactured by the very same companies.

While purists may, with good reason, still prefer to make their own granola, the distinctions are blurring for the general public. The corporate giants who give America its bleached white flour and chemical-rich cake mixes also offer consumers wheat germ and natural vitamins, as well as more and more products labeled "everything natural, nothing artificial."

All of this is very confusing. Is the fast food customer who sprinkles alfalfa sprouts onto a grilled hot dog really a health food fan after all? Despite their vulnerability to bugs, grubs, and fungus infections are organically grown fruits, vegetables, and cereal grains really that much better for us? What's wrong with the high sugar content of cookies, cupcakes, and candy bars, the salt and the fat in potato chips? What are the chemicals we hear so much about that are added to our food, and why can't we trust our government to see that only the "safe" ones get to us?

What *can* we eat in America today that isn't nutritionally a fake, fattening, bad for our teeth, cancer-threatening or otherwise dangerous to our health—and that still tastes good?

PART
1

FROM HOME-GROWN TO MASS PRODUCED

1 HOW AMERICA ATE BEFORE 1900

Things were much simpler in the days when America was younger and its food choices were far fewer than they are today. No one spoke of "junk food" or "health food" in the Virginia colony during the dreadful winter of 1609–1610 known as the "starving time." No Kentucky pioneer breaking virgin ground for a cornpatch in the 1790s, no mountain man stalking bear and beaver in the Rockies in the 1830s, ever dreamed of convenience foods like "instant" this and "minute" that. And no sodbusting farmer of the Great Plains in the 1880s ever gave any thought as to whether he was growing his crops organically (although almost certainly he was).

WHEN PEOPLE ATE VITTLES

"Vittles" were what most people ate. The word was a popular adaptation of victuals, which meant nourishment, provisions, that which was necessary to sustain human life. Scouts, frontiersmen, soldiers, and cowboys had even shorter and more direct words for their food—chow, grub, mess, and chuck.

Almost all the foods our forebears ate were, of course, natural foods in that they were grown and raised without artificial fertilizers, feeds, sprays, or injections. They were also—to use another term we hear nowadays—whole foods, for they were not factory processed or much tampered with between the time they left the field or the barnyard, the waters or the woodlands, and the time they reached the family dinner table.

Colonial and pioneer Americans did, however, have an assortment of *naturally* processed convenience foods that served to carry farm families through the long winters, when few fresh foods were available, and to provision explorers and hunters on long journeys into the wilderness.

Jerky—thin strips of sun-dried or smoke-dried venison or other game—was a survival gift from the Indians. Leathery and chewy though it was, it offered high-quality protein nutriment when all else failed. The Pennsylvania Dutch (really German settlers of the late 1600s) used a drying process to preserve the apples and pears of their carefully tended orchards. Cut into slices known as *Schnitz*, these fruits were dried in the late-summer sun or in the fading heat of bake ovens. They kept without spoiling and could be used all winter in pies and other dishes. When soaked in water, the dried apples for a *Schnitz* pie became plump and juicy once again.

Salt and spices were age-old preservatives that provided convenience foods for Americans during the first three hundred years of settlement and expansion. New Englanders "corned" beef. They put it to soak in a pickling mixture of salt and peppercorns, which retarded spoilage, flavored and tenderized the meat, and kept it on hand for a boiled dinner when fresh-killed meat was not available. Southerners used a similar technique with pork. They salted and then smoke-cured hams, bacon, and other hog-butchering cuts.

Certain vegetables could be preserved by immersing them in a spicy brine mixture. Cucumbers became pickles;

cabbage became sauerkraut. And what farm family would have tried to get along without a root cellar? In those cool earthen dugouts, root and tuberous vegetables like onions, potatoes, beets, carrots, parsnips, turnips, and rutabagas could be kept without rotting from one season's harvesting to the next.

All these convenience foods used in the farmhouse kitchens of America's past—sun-dried, smoke-cured, salted, pickled, or cold-storaged—came directly from nature and were processed by nature or with natural ingredients. The words "nothing artificial" truly applied to them.

As for fast foods, a ripe blackberry plucked from a bush, or a mellow, flame-colored persimmon taken from a tree just tinged with frost were certainly fast in their journey from source to mouth. Of course, one's timing needed to be just right. It had to be in harmony with nature's timing. But then, the pace of life was much slower in the pre-twentieth-century United States, and nobody had yet thought of going around with a stopwatch to time the preparation of a hamburger or a taco from a fast food eatery.

FROM CANNING TO FREEZING

Changes in the food picture were beginning to take place though. Canned foods were already on the scene by the 1840s in the United States, and the Civil War spurred the production of the long-keeping containers of tomatoes, pork-and-beans, sauerkraut, and fruits that were so useful in feeding the armies. The heat-sealing preserving process that killed bacteria had been invented in the early 1800s by a Frenchman, Nicolas Appert, to supply troops in Napoleon's wars. Having determined that air caused food to spoil, Appert developed the idea of putting hot, cooked food into glass jars, which he corked, heated again in boiling water, and sealed with sealing wax. Soon after, tin cans invented in England were adopted for use by commercial canners.

Canned evaporated milk also appeared in the mid-1800s. Cooking off more than half the water content of milk to reduce its volume, and canning the result, was the work of Gail Borden, whose name later lent itself to a large dairy company. Canned milk, sanitary and safe, was welcomed in the 1850s and 1860s by the growing number of American city dwellers who could no longer keep cows and were at the mercy of dairy farmers who added water to the milk they sold. Grim humorists said that if the dairyman's well went dry, he would have to go out of business!

Worse, the dairymen's cows were often diseased, even tubercular, for many were fed city garbage or brewery slops, and milking conditions were unsanitary. Pasteurization—heating fresh milk to a high temperature to kill harmful bacteria—was not widely practiced in American cities until the late 1890s.

So the growth of cities during the nineteenth century, as well as the demands of wartime troop feeding, helped bring about the earliest type of commercial food processing—canning.

Refrigeration, with artifically made ice, was another method of food preservation developed during the 1800s. Its first use, starting in 1868, was in railroad refrigerator cars that brought beef carcasses east from Chicago and other meat-slaughtering centers, and that also gave Americans their first taste of out-of-season and nonregional fruits and vegetables grown in warmer parts of the country.

As most city people no longer had root cellars for cold storage, home iceboxes modeled on the refrigerated railroad-car idea grew in popularity after the Civil War. In the past, only wealthy Southerners with large numbers of slaves had enjoyed the luxury of an "icehouse" that provided chilled drinks and frozen desserts. The icehouses of the Southern planters had required natural ice that had to be laboriously cut and transported, and then stored in well-insulated underground shelters for warm-weather use.

Thanks to the invention of artificial ice-making the squat wooden icebox, with its wide-mouthed basin underneath to catch the drippings of the melted ice, saw most American families into the early years of the twentieth century. Fresh milk, butter, vegetables, and meats could now be kept on hand for several days in houses and apartments that not only lacked a cold cellar but had a furnace in the basement for central heating.

Summer and winter, the iceman was a frequent visitor who had to be told how many blocks or pounds of ice were needed at each delivery. The ice was usually placed in an upper compartment of the icebox, so that the rising warm air would be cooled and then circulate downward. The water from the melting ice trickled out through a pipe. And what household during those decades didn't experience the panic of the overflowing catch basin and the flooded kitchen floor!

Automatic home refrigerators, of the kind in use today, didn't come along before the 1920s. And rural families who had no electricity had to wait for such refrigerators until the 1930s and 1940s.

Long-keeping dehydrated foods arrived on the scene as early as the turn of the century. Jell-O, the forerunner of hundreds of quick-mix dry products of the "just add water" variety, made its appearance in 1897. Almost at once, it found a place on the American pantry shelf and came to be considered healthful and wholesome, the perfect treat for generations of children, invalids, dieters, and everybody else.

A closer look at Jell-O and its fellow gelatin mixes in recent years, however, reveals that these desserts are low in nutrition and high in sugar and synthetic additives. For behind their sparkle, they contain only 10 percent gelatin (which offers a poor quality protein, in any case), 85 percent refined sugar, and an array of artificial flavors and colors.

Yet Americans of the early 1900s quickly bought Jell-O's tinted-sugar success formula that was to serve as the model for many other sugar-laden, coal-tar-dye colored, imitation fruit-flavored products, particularly powdered and liquid soft drinks, confections, and frozen desserts.

Freezing, still another way of processing food for long keeping, grew out of the principles of automatic refrigeration. Soon it came to rival canning.

The process of freezing began when a Brooklyn-born inventor named Clarence Birdseye noticed, during a trip to Labrador in the early 1900s, that fish taken from the sea in subfreezing temperatures and quick-frozen by nature tasted almost as good as fresh when thawed and cooked. Birdseye discovered that mechanical flash freezing rather than slow freezing was the key to preventing tissue breakdown, and the process that he patented in the 1920s set the scene for the vast frozen-food industry that exists today.

By the 1950s, American families had added a new kind of "pantry shelf," the home freezer or refrigerator freezing compartment, for storing both home-prepared and store-bought frozen foods. Freezers made it possible to have all sorts of fruits and vegetables (most of which tasted better than canned) available all year round. Freezers also meant less frequent trips to the store, and permitted quantity buying and cooking that saved both money and time.

Not surprisingly, freezing also put new kinds of commercially prepared foods on the American dinner table, including TV dinners, chicken and beef potpies, sauced noodle and rice concoctions, and many other cooked or partly cooked frozen entrees. Even though a more careful look at these foods has revealed that they are of questionable value in terms of cost, taste, and nutrition, consumers responded enthusiastically to their "convenience."

The arrival of canning, refrigeration, freezing, and sophisticated food processing signaled great advances for American food technology. No one could dispute the advantages of automatic refrigerators and home freezers. But, on the other hand, few people ever questioned the growing use of synthetic substitutes for real food flavors, textures, and colors. In fact, "everything artificial, nothing natural" might well have been the slogan of the food chemists who developed Jell-O in 1897, and of those who were soon to follow them. And the public probably would have applauded that slogan.

2 TWENTIETH-CENTURY FOOD TECHNOLOGY

If the turn of the century heralded the appearance of chemical substitutes from the food laboratory, it also opened the era of scientific food preparation in the home.

The credit for telling American cooks exactly how many tablespoons of butter and how many cups of flour to measure off for a recipe—and for standardizing those measurements—generally goes to Fanny Farmer, whose *Boston Cooking-School Cook Book* was published in 1896. The cooking school itself, something quite new in the United States, had been established in 1879. And Miss Farmer, the "mother of level measurements," became its principal in 1891. The Boston Cooking School, in calling its course of study "domestic science," aptly reflected the new relationship between food and science.

The year 1901 saw the publication of another cookbook, a 174-page recipe collection based on cooking lessons given to immigrant settlers in Milwaukee, Wisconsin, at a community center known as The Settlement House. Its title was *The Way to a Man's Heart . . . The Settlement Cook Book*, for it was assumed in those days that only women were supposed to cook, and that they did so almost exclusively for the approval of men. In any case, The Settlement House, too, aimed to convert cooking by "pinches" and "handfuls" into cooking by accurate measurements. At the same time, it tried to acquaint newcomers from other cultures with American ingredients and with the preparation of American dishes.

As the years went by, both Fanny Farmer's and The Settlement House's cookbooks went into dozens of frequently revised editions, selling copies in the millions, and many other basic, instructional cookbooks appeared. The clamor for cookbooks showed that the hog-and-hominy-eating days of the old frontier were just about over. People wanted a little more delicacy in their dishes and a little more imagination in their meals. Besides, there were new products around that heralded the food technology being advanced by industrial science. And cookbooks told how to prepare fancy salads and desserts molded in gelatin, how to use baking powder and the new solid white vegetable shortenings in cakes and quickbreads, and how to convert the new canned soups into sauces for "creamed" fish and poultry entrees. Synthetic additives, such as the artificial flavorings, colorings, and preservatives in many of these foods weren't considered bad or dangerous; they were the results of scientific research. And science was the new god in the kitchen.

LEARNING ABOUT NUTRITION

Nutrition and dietetics were also brand new scientific ideas in the early 1900s. In the past, nobody had thought about balancing proteins, carbohydrates, and fats in their diet, or worried much about getting enough vitamins and minerals. The identification of vitamin substances didn't even begin until the early decades of the twentieth century, even though rickets, scurvy, and beriberi—all vitamin deficiency diseases—had been health scourges for centuries.

Following the discovery of vitamin C, orange juice and

grapefruit made their first appearances on the American breakfast table. Soon there was a growing demand for all sorts of fresh produce, and since it had to be shipped long distances by rail across the expanding nation, growers began to develop varieties of citrus fruits, peaches, and tomatoes that could be picked firm and unripe. If they didn't taste quite as good as tree-ripened, they were also hardy and squash-proof. The American public accepted them as still another achievement of the twentieth century.

Through the new study of dietetics, Americans were also beginning to learn about calories—those little energy units in food that could add up to excessive body fat—and, by the 1920s, they were actually beginning to go on reducing diets.

About half the population now lived in towns or cities, many people worked in offices and at other sedentary jobs, and they needed fewer calories than if they had been engaged in physical labor. Also the new fashions for women dictated the pencil-slim, flat-chested, flapper look. Insurance companies began to warn of the health dangers of overweight, and breakfasts and lunches, in particular, became lighter.

Steak, corned-beef hash, hotbreads, pie, and other staples of the lumber camp, ranch, or farmhouse breakfast were abolished in favor of the new ready-to-eat dry cereals that had been created by the Kellogg brothers of Battle Creek, Michigan, and others during the last quarter of the nineteenth century. Lunches, too, shrank as city office workers and ambitious businessmen, pressed for time, took up the custom of the quick lunch eaten from a counter stool.

New cookbooks offering slimming diets appeared, as well as a chewing technique advocated by a man named Horace

Fletcher, who was himself obese. The technique, known as Fletcherism, consisted of chewing each mouthful slowly until it was nearly liquid. Fletcherism was intended, in part, to remedy the effects of the hasty grabbing, gobbling, and gulping of food that had long characterized American eating. Dyspepsia, or indigestion, was said to be the national malady of the United States, and the public spent a small fortune on patented remedies to relieve stomach distress. Fletcherism was also considered beneficial in helping the overweight cut down on their food intake, as slower chewing tended to bring on a feeling of stomach fullness. So Americans began their long battle with their waistlines.

PACKAGING AND THE SUPERMARKET EXPLOSION

The struggle for slimness and health in twentieth-century America was destined to be difficult, its way beset with temptation. For food was becoming the province of big business, and the food companies were beginning to learn a new technique for luring the shopper: packaging.

In the beginning, the products inside the enticing-looking new packages weren't necessarily new. In 1899, Uneeda biscuits, which had always been sold in bulk from a cracker barrel in the general store, were put into a cardboard box at the factory. The new package was more than a wrapping, though; it was also an advertisement that would lead to much bigger sales and profits.

Little by little the large wooden tubs of butter, waist-high pails of milk, crates of eggs, huge burlap sacks of dried peas and beans, and of sugar, tea, and coffee beans began to vanish from the corner grocery store and to be replaced by individual take-home cartons, bottles, boxes, bags, or other containers bearing brand names. Even ice cream, most of which continued to be sold in bulk through the 1930s, had already appeared packaged in 1921 in the form of the Eskimo Pie, a rectangular mold of vanilla ice cream enclosed in a chocolate coating.

There was no question that the prepackaging of food was more sanitary and convenient, and established a uniformity of product. At the same time, however, the package added to the cost of the food, and food companies soon capitalized on this principle by charging more per ounce for smaller packages. Careful shoppers have since learned, however, that it isn't *always* true that the "large, economy size" is a better buy.

Today package design is a major aspect of the food business. The package serves not only to identify the product and to develop customer loyalty to a certain brand, but also to catch the eye and appeal to the appetite. It can do even more. It can create and sell something that nobody would otherwise buy. For example, back in the days of the old-fashioned cracker-barrel grocery store, would anybody have paid good money for a handful of dried noodles and a few pinches of dehydrated sauce-and-seasoning mixture? Yet these are the ingredients, sold at a price far beyond their value, of a packaged product called Hamburger Helper to which the consumer must add the costliest ingredient—ground meat. But the steaming, tasty-looking, full-color dish on the package creates and sells an *idea* for food rather than the food itself. The packaging, in this case, probably costs the food company *more* than the contents of the package. But the company doesn't mind. The cost can easily be passed on to the consumer.

There are hundreds of food mixes on today's grocery shelves that could not be sold without their expert packaging designs. Take that stack of hot, fluffy pancakes, topped with melting butter and drenched in syrup, on the package of pancake mix; or the golden, moist-crumbed, chocolate-frosted layer cake on the cake-mix box. Of course, the consumer must supply the butter, the pancake syrup, the cake frosting (possibly from another mix), and the eggs that go into the batters. The expensive mixes themselves are little more than ordinary flour and, of course, additives from the food laboratories.

It's almost a rule, in fact, that the more processed the product, the more colorful and inviting the package. The drabbest-looking items on the supermarket shelves are those plain cardboard boxes or plastic bags of dried peas and beans, those double-thickness paper sacks of flour and sugar. And unless you've come to the store with a specific intention to buy one of these basic foods, they are not likely to attract your eye or to incite you to what is known as impulse buying.

Nor could impulse buying, that archenemy of wallets and waistlines, ever have come into its own without the development of the self-service store and eventually the supermarket.

At the old-time grocery store, people came to buy what they needed and not much else. If some dried fruit or the new season's crop of hazelnuts had just come in, they might add a pound or two of those to their order. Each customer, of course, had to be waited on by a clerk who went back and forth weighing and wrapping each item. Often the customer brought along a market basket for carrying home the smaller purchases, while heavy items were sent on later by horse and wagon.

Early versions of the self-service grocery store and the in-store shopping basket or wheeled cart signaled changes to come. In 1916, a store called Piggly Wiggly opened in Memphis, Tennessee. It was the forerunner of a chain that was later to spread into a number of other states. Customers entered through a turnstile and walked through aisles from which they could select the prepackaged items of the day. As shortages of help developed with the United States' entry into World War I, the new system requiring fewer store clerks was looked on with favor.

But the nation wasn't quite ready for the supermarket in the 1920s. Food shopping was still being done on an almost daily basis, and full-service corner stores—either independently owned or like those of the famous A&P chain—were the most convenient. The A&P, which had started in 1859 as a tea-importing company with a single store in Lower Manhattan, New York, had developed into a 15,000-unit chain by 1930. The chain store idea had proved a success in itself, offering customers a nationwide reputation for reliability and economy, for the chains presumably passed on the savings of their quantity wholesale buying.

The conversion of small clerk-behind-the-counter grocery stores into supermarkets did not really begin until the late 1930s. World War II, however, with its tightened consumer supplies and food rationing, interrupted the development of the new, big-scale, self-service store. But by the early 1950s, the sleek, modern supermarket had begun to come into its own. More Americans now owned automatic refrigerators and freezers. Better food storage facilities in the home meant shopping could be done once or twice weekly. And the greater traveling distance to the supermarket didn't matter that much because more people now owned automobiles.

Of course, the independent corner grocery store, with its mixture of bulk and packaged foods, its credit and delivery services, and its generally higher prices would be around for a while. But the days of most such "mom and pop" operations, so called because they were family-owned and family-run, were clearly numbered.

THE NEW TECHNOLOGY

In the course of a few decades of the twentieth century, a revolutionary change had taken place in the American food supply and in the way Americans ate. As recently as the year 1900, two out of every three Americans still lived on farms. They could actually watch their food sprouting, grazing, or hopping about just outside the farmhouse window. And in the farmhouse kitchen, families still used mostly natural or naturally processed foods and ate cooked-from-scratch meals. Today, with only 3 to 4 percent of the United States population directly engaged in agriculture, very few of us are intimate with our food sources, and most of us have been lured by the flashier, factory-processed enticements of the supermarket shelves and the fast food chains.

We sometimes wonder whether Americans *asked* for more mass-produced, longer-keeping, highly processed food or whether food technologists and big business simply got together and decided to give it to us. This is a little like trying to find out about the chicken and the egg: which came first? For scientific and industrial progress on the food front was an outgrowth of the Industrial Revolution. And society, in turn, was destined to be transformed by the new technology.

As the Industrial Revolution also led to the growth of cities, to reduced farming acreage, to fewer people working the land and more people than ever to feed, it soon became necessary to develop more efficient and intensive methods of food production. Here, too, the new technology stepped in, with more sophisticated farm machinery, chemical fertilizers, and other aids.

Unfortunately, progress in agricultural techniques has also led to overkill and ruthlessness, as in the use of crop insecticides that disrupt the balance of nature and the feeding of livestock with cancer-causing growth hormones. Commercial food processors, too, engage in many questionable practices, such as adding chemical substances of known or suspected danger to our food, like the sodium nitrite in frankfurters and bologna, the saccharin in diet sodas, and the synthetic dyes that seem to color almost everything we eat.

WEIGHING PAST AND PRESENT

Because the twentieth century seems to have brought with it so many food curses along with its blessings, many people speak glowingly of the "good old days." Let's take a final glance backward. Was the food of colonial and pioneer America really better—tastier, more wholesome, more varied?

We can only guess at some of the answers. Reports about how the food of the past tasted are highly subjective, especially as they have most often come to us from the hungry or the homesick, or from the occasional foreign visitor intrigued with the offerings of the exotic new continent. In truth, much American food of the seventeenth to nineteenth centuries would probably not appeal to our taste buds today. Meats and fowl usually had a strong, gamey flavor and were chewy and tough, wild fruits and berries were for the most part tart and acid-tasting, and corncakes baked in an open fireplace were gritty with ash. Soups and stews were greasy, vegetables were overcooked and often swam in hog fat, and puddings were leaden. The wholesomeness of the foods of our forebears must also be examined with honesty. Foods in their natural state can, in some cases, be as dangerous, if not more so, as some of the synthetic substances on which we feast today. Untreated grains can grow toxic molds that cause hallucinations, even death, and natural manures used as fertilizer can contaminate foods with harmful bacteria, bringing on nausea, vomiting, and diarrhea.

Poisonous berries, mushrooms, and wild young greens were responsible for many frontier deaths, and botulism— the deadliest of all bacterial food poisons—was an ever-present threat that lurked in the home-canned foods of the farmhouse pantry.

As to variety, the food of the American past did include an abundance of local and regional specialties. Each household produced its own breads and other baked goods, hams, cider, and cheeses, and each was unique. Also, before the onset of mass production and standardization, numerous varieties of apples, pears, berries, and other fruits and vegetables were cultivated across the country. But few people could travel the entire land sampling all of these local varieties, so for the individual family or community the range of accessible food was, in fact, very limited.

To glorify the American food of past centuries by heaping it with unqualified praise, while damning the food of the present, would obviously be a mistake. Like today's food, it probably ranked from commendable to awful. But most of it, at least, appears to have been honest food that, at its best, was responsible for a number of nutritious and mouth-watering dishes. The contemporary food scene, dominated by our twentieth-century terminology, represents a sharp break with the past. Yet, an unbiased look at how we ate then and how we eat today may help us to choose a future course that reflects the very best from the entire spectrum of American eating.

PART 2

EATING IN AMERICA TODAY

1 SWEET TREATS AND SALTY SNACKS

Devil Dogs or Twinkies, Froot Loops or Sugar Smacks, M&Ms or Screaming Yellow Zonkers—what's your favorite sugar-charged junk food? Or do you get your kicks from salty snacks—Chee-tos, Fritos, popcorn, or potato chips? Happy wanderers in the junk food jungle, high on the caffeine in cola drinks, or tranquilized by the hand-to-mouth mechanics of eating one "taco-flavored" tortilla chip after another, most of us don't even want to escape.

Why should we? Everything that appeals to our taste buds seems to be right here. And it isn't only those overstimulated sugar-sensitive and salt-sensitive zones on our tongues that are so happy with junk food. Crispy and crunchy, creamy-smooth, icy-cold, chewy, mellow, tangy, or zingy—junk food also supplies a wide range of wonderful mouth sensations. And, if the food companies suspect we might be getting tired of the old sensations, they are always ready to come up with a new taste treat or texture thrill, such as chewing gum pellets with liquid centers that "spurt" flavor, or candies that "explode" in your mouth!

For some of our top-notch junk foods, sugar and salt are backed up by fats and/or starches. Doughnuts are a prime example of a sugar-fat-*and*-starch combination, while sweetened dry cereals typify the pairing of sugar and starch, and ice cream that of sugar and fat (plus air). For those irresistible salted snacks, salt is wedded to corn, potatoes, nuts, or flour, and large amounts of fat are usually present, too.

With all the junk food that is hauled home from supermarkets, gulped down in fast food eateries, and that comes clunking and gushing out of vending machines, we shouldn't be surprised to learn that Americans annually consume, on the average, 100 pounds of refined sugar, 125 pounds of fat, and up to 25 times more salt than the human body requires. These figures come from recent studies reported by the U.S. Senate Select Committee on Nutrition and Human Needs.

Sugar and salt are not basically harmful substances. But eaten in excess, they become distinct health dangers. Refined sugar is a carbohydrate that supplies 113 calories per ounce but is totally lacking in vitamins, minerals, and other important nutritive factors. Too much sugar can cause tooth decay and obesity, and increase the likelihood of diabetes. Foods high in sugar also rob the body of good nutrition for they substitute "empty" calories—lacking in essential proteins, vitamins, and minerals—for those of more healthful foods.

Salt can raise the blood pressure, and may lead to hypertension and stroke. Fat, while it is a basic nutritional need, varies in quality according to its source. Too much fat is directly related to overweight and, depending on the type of fat and how the body handles it, is linked to cancer and heart disease. And the starches used in junk foods are usually highly processed, and therefore parted from their important micronutrients and from their fiber content—the roughage in plant foods that is beneficial to the human digestive tract.

THE SUGAR IN OUR LIVES

Sugar! Just visualize gobbling up the contents of 20 of those hefty 5-pound bags that are heaped on the shelves of your local supermarket. However, that isn't quite the way it happens. Most of the 100 pounds of sucrose (refined cane or beet sugar) that Americans swallow each year doesn't come directly out of bags of sugar brought home from the store. About 70 percent of it comes to us in the processed foods we buy—from candies to ketchup, cereals to canned soups, soft drinks to salad dressings. Yes, even foods that don't taste the least bit sweet, like canned vegetables or salted snack foods, often have refined sugar (or corn syrup or other sweeteners) added to them.

Food processing really does put more sugar in our lives. Back in the first decade of the twentieth century, Americans consumed only about two-thirds the amount of sucrose per person that they do today. And less than 20 percent of it came from processed foods, simply because a lot of baking, preserving, and canning was still being done at home.

Although we're now eating more sugar than we ever have—the most ever eaten in human history—we could get along with a lot less than even our great-great-grandparents consumed. For sugars occur naturally in many foods, such as milk (where the sugar is called lactose) and honey and fruits (where the sugars are glucose, fructose, and sucrose). Sugars result, too, from the digestive breakdown of starches in our bodies.

History has proved that people can live perfectly well without any refined sugar at all. The western world knew nothing about sugar until the armies of Alexander the Great trekked from Greece to India in the fourth century B.C. and found what was described as a "hard honey," grainy as salt but sweet in taste, that "grew" on tall canes. Up until then, honey was the main sweetener in most parts of the world. And it continued in that role for many more centuries, until after the discovery of the New World and the cultivation of sugar in the Americas.

When the first Europeans reached Mexico in the early 1500s, they found the Aztecs using chocolate as the basis of a dark, bitter, spicy sauce for turkey. Sugar was, of course, unknown, and the Indians of the Americas had never dreamed of combining their ground cacao beans with anything sweet so that they could eat chocolate as a confection! Even today, in many nonindustrialized societies, refined sugar and processed sweets are little known, and meals do not end with dessert. Groups of misguided tourists who distribute "bonbons" to children in remote African villages do not stop to think that they may be handing out the pain of toothaches to communities that have no dental care.

How then did the human "sweet tooth," with its escalating demands, develop? The answer lies in our conditioning, both as a society and as individuals. We can all remember how, as small children, we were offered sweets as a reward for having finished all our broccoli, or as a consolation to help dry our tears. Sugar simply tasted good, and the more we got the more we wanted. Some nutritionists believe that sugar is addictive because it is an "incomplete" food, and therefore we have a higher tolerance level for it than we do for foods that supply necessary nutrients. This tolerance can become a craving.

JUNK FLUIDS

The craving for sweets is all too generously accommodated in twentieth-century America. Junk fluids—sodas and other soft drinks—contribute *most* of the sugar we get from processed foods, nearly 25 percent of it. Each year the average American downs 36 gallons of carbonated beverages alone. That doesn't include all the noncarbonated soft drinks that are low in natural fruit juices and high in sugar content, preservatives, and artificial colorings and flavorings. According to our federal labeling laws, a "juice drink" does not have to have more than 50 percent natural juice in it, an "ade" need have only 25 percent, and a "drink" only 10 percent. There are many orange-juice substitutes with fancy health and flavor claims, but unless the label says "100 percent orange juice" it isn't the real thing.

Artificial colorings in soft drinks do even more than artificial flavorings in influencing our taste buds. Grape drinks are colored purple, lemon drinks yellow, and lime drinks green, even though most natural fruit juices range from pale to nearly colorless. In an interesting experiment in which artificial flavors and colors were wrongly paired, many of the volunteer tasters made errors, such as mistaking lemon for cherry because the drink was colored bright red. And the memory of natural fruit flavors fades as we are deluged with more and more artificial versions. Natural fruit flavors are altered, too, by processing which results, for example, in the "tin can" taste of pineapple, orange, and grapefruit juice that some people have actually come to prefer.

Powdered "fruit" drinks like Kool-Aid and Tang have been steadily growing in popularity because of their convenience. The earliest crude, dehydrated concentrates appeared about fifty years ago, but their formulas weren't too successful at first. Today's instant-mix packets of sugar and chemicals require only water from the kitchen sink for transformation into a smooth liquid. A few do come unsweetened so that you can add your own sugar, but the artificial additives are still part of the package.

Soda pop, of course, can't be concentrated into a crystalline powder because it contains air. Its invention goes back to the late 1700s when Joseph Priestley, an English scientist, succeeded in making a bubbling water similar to the gaseous waters that came from certain natural mineral springs. In the United States, by the mid-1800s, lemon, ginger, sarsaparilla and other root flavorings (often called root beer) were being added to plain soda water, along with sugar of course.

Cola-flavored drinks were first attempted in the 1880s. The Coca-Cola, Pepsi-Cola, and other colas that account for 60 percent of the soda pop sold today contain a syrup made from the kola nut, plus natural and artificial flavorings and colorings. Caffeine, a stimulant found in coffee and tea, is also present in kola nuts, which come from a tree grown in the tropics. As the caffeine in the kola nut is partly lost in the processing, cola formulas contain additional caffeine as well—the very same caffeine that coffee companies have removed from decaffeinated coffee!

That pepped-up feeling that makes some cola-drinking children strangely hyperactive doesn't come from the "zippy" carbonation or from the "quick energy" provided by the sugar, but from the same substance that can keep coffee-drinking adults turning and tossing through a sleepless night. Even Dr. Pepper, one of the non-cola-flavored soda pops, contains caffeine.

For soda-drinkers who don't want a caffeine "high," there are popular lemon-lime drinks without caffeine, like Seven-Up. But the high sugar content is still there, providing nearly 100 calories for every 8 ounces, just as in most colas and other soft drinks.

Beverage manufacturers have a solution to that problem, too. For those who would like to lower their calorie intake, they offer "diet" drinks containing saccharin, an artificial sweetener that is hundreds of times sweeter than sugar yet contains no calories. Diet Seven-Up and the artificial-citrus drink called Fresca (which is manufactured by the Coca-Cola company) have only 2 calories in every 8-ounce glass, while Diet Pepsi has only one calorie per 12 ounces and Coca-Cola's Tab has one calorie for every 16 ounces.

Saccharin, also known as sodium saccharin, was synthesized in the laboratory in 1879 and has been used commercially since 1900. It has long been considered a special boon to people with diabetes, who have a low tolerance for sugar. But in recent years saccharin has come under sharp scrutiny. A laboratory study sponsored by the Canadian government has shown that saccharin causes bladder cancer in rats. While it is believed that the daily intake would have to be very large to have a similar effect on humans, the possibility cannot be ruled out. And there may be special risks for children whose mothers were saccharin users and who, in turn, begin to consume saccharin from an early age. About 35 percent of children under the age of ten are believed to be regular users of saccharin.

The federal outlawing of saccharin would probably bring some new laboratory-created sweetener onto the scene, not unlike the cyclamates that appeared in 1950 to rival saccharin because the latter has a slightly bitter aftertaste. By 1970, however, cyclamates had been banned because they were proved to have caused birth abnormalities in baby chicks and bladder cancer in rats. Assessing the long-term effects of a new product takes time, so while a successor to saccharin might appear to be safe, it too might later come to be regarded as a health menace.

Nearly 75 percent of the saccharin Americans have been consuming since 1970 has been in low-calorie soft drinks. But the chemical sweetener also turns up in other products like sugarless gum, mouthwash, toothpaste, and diet desserts, and has been highly popular as a tabletop sweetener for coffee and tea. Despite warnings on saccharin labels stating that the substance may be hazardous to health, the public's enthusiasm for this convenience chemical has not abated, and saccharin users have strongly opposed an outright ban.

One of the big problems with sugar substitutes of any kind is that they seem to do nothing to cut down the desire for sweets. They may, in fact, increase it. Just think of all those would-be dieters who drink a can of low-calorie Tab or put Sweet 'n Low in their coffee so they can feel free to load up on layer cake, cream pie, chocolate mousse, or some other high-calorie dessert.

SUGARBOWL BREAKFASTS

After soft drinks, breakfast cereals and commercial baked goods are the processed foods that dump the largest dosage of sugar into our diets. Most of us would feel somewhat guilty about eating frosted cupcakes for breakfast, but what about all those "nourishing, fortified, vitamin-enriched" dry cereals, those frosted crisps, cocoa-flavored puffs, and fruited crunches, many of which contain more than 50 percent sugar? Some have been found to have a sugar content of nearly 70 percent, and even those healthful-sounding commercial granola cereals are in the 15 to 20 percent sugar category.

You can't tell the percentage of sugar in a presweetened cereal simply by reading the label because federal law requires only that the most plentiful ingredient be listed first, the next most plentiful second, and so on. Many of the "sugarbowl" breakfast cereals that began appearing on our tables in the late 1940s actually have more sugar in them than milk-chocolate candy! Yet young children who are captives of TV entertainment are persuaded by friendly cartoon tigers and cuddly bears, smiling astronauts and jolly pirates, package prizes and other "giveaways," to demand these breakfast foods from their parents. The manufacturers of these low-nutrition but high-profit cereals are ensuring their own futures for, as they know all too well, the eating habits and food preferences acquired in the early years tend to stay with people all their lives.

Not too surprisingly, sugary cereals, especially the crunchier kinds, cause as many cavities as the sweet, chewy candy bars that Americans have adored for nearly a century. Today about half of the adult population of the United States is toothless by age fifty-five, although dentures hide this fact from our general view, and 98 percent of children have tooth decay. With so many younger Americans now eating an extra share of concentrated sugar in the morning, *their* teeth may not even last them into their fifties.

LUNCHBOX TREATS

Following a sugary breakfast, many children go off to school with a lunchbox containing Twinkies, Oreos,

Chip-A-Roos, or some other treat from International Telephone and Telegraph's Continental Baking Division, Nabisco (National Biscuit Company), or Sunshine Biscuits—giants among the commercial bakers that supply supermarket shelves with packaged cakes and cookies. If the chocolate in some of these school-lunch desserts isn't real and if the "creme" filling is really just sugar and shortening, who's to know? Most young children have never tasted the real thing and couldn't recognize the difference. They are contented with the overriding flavor, which is that of sweetness.

Big-scale commercial cookie baking in America began around the turn of the century when a number of local and regional bakeries were merged to form the National Biscuit Company. Ginger Snaps, Animal Crackers, and Fig Newtons were among the favorites in those days, with the layered, wafflelike Sugar Wafers considered special party fare because of the extra-sweet icing between the layers.

Oreos, the classic "creme" sandwich, came along in 1912. Sunshine Biscuits, which also began baking in the early years of the century, soon imitated Nabisco's chocolate Oreo with its similar Hydrox cookie. Over the years, both companies introduced sweeter and richer packaged cookies, especially the candylike chocolate-chip and chocolate-coated varieties, far different from the plain Arrowroots, Social Teas, and Lorna Doones that once satisfied the American sweet tooth.

When it comes to commercially distributed cakes, whether they are packaged creme-filled cupcakes from the supermarket, freshly baked fast food doughnuts, or fancy dessert cakes from the deep freeze, all are nutritionally similar. They are all high in refined sugar, bleached white flour, and saturated fats. Commercial baked goods also include dough conditioners, mold inhibitors, stabilizers, moisturizers, thickeners, emulsifiers, and other additives to assure a long shelf life, an unvarying product, an attractive appearance, or whatever else is required. Not all additives are known to be dangerous and not all additives are artificial. But some are used to deceive us into thinking a product is better than it is, and we really know very little about the cumulative and interactive effects of additives once inside the human body.

When American families gave up home baking, or turned to baking from mixes, they lost control of both the quality and quantity of the ingredients used. While it could be argued that home-baked cakes and cookies made with refined sugar are junk food, too, the home baker *can* cut down on the amount of sugar used. In most recipes, sweetening can be reduced by as much as one-fourth, and the flavor and texture will actually be better. Even so-called natural-ingredient commercial baked goods tend to contain a great deal of sugar in proportion to their other ingredients. The home baker can also include whole wheat rather than white flour in some recipes, use polyunsaturated fats instead of the less healthful saturated types, and no synthetic chemical additives other than leavening agents.

STRAIGHT SUGAR

If soft drinks, heavily presweetened cereals, and most cakes, cookies, pies, and doughnuts qualify as junk food, candy earns the junk food crown in terms of its high concentration of sugar and its low quotient of other nutritional ingredients such as eggs, flour, grains, fruits, or even water. Even the peanuts, wheat germ, and other "health food" items with which manufacturers try to redeem candy bars nowadays are canceled out by the dominance of sugar.

The sugar may be present in the form of corn syrup or invert sugar (sucrose that has been broken down into glucose and fructose) for the purpose of preventing crystallization and retaining moisture, depending on the type of candy. For the American confectionery scene ranges from hard sucking candies, the "boiled sweets" of English colonial influence, to the chocolate bars that were developed in small candy kitchens during the early decades of the twentieth century.

There really was a Peter Paul Halajian, an Ethel and Frank Mars, and a Milton Hershey who pioneered the Peter Paul Mounds, Mars' Milky Ways, and Hershey Almond Bars that are best-selling commercial confectionery products today.

The "country fresh" butter and cream and "real chocolate" that once made candy-eating seem a little less sinful have fallen victim to the high cost of those ingredients in recent years. As candy-bar sizes have shrunk and prices have risen, cheap saturated fats, synthetic chocolate flavorings, and a host of additives have come into use. Unless chocolate candy is made with a product of the cacao bean, including its fat which is called cocoa butter, it just isn't real chocolate.

The basic ingredient of chewing gum has also gone from natural to artificial. Chicle, a latex or gummy juice from the sapodilla tree that grows from Mexico to South America, is not the only substance in the "gum base" of your favorite, sugar-coated stick, wad, or pellet. Gum-base additives such as synthetic "plasticizers" and "elasticizers" are not listed on the label. And the gum base may, in fact, be wholly synthetic, just like the artificial flavorings, colorings, and freshness preservers in the gum.

Chewing gum isn't new. The ancient Greeks chewed on sticky resins obtained from the mastic tree, the Mayan Indians chewed natural chicle, and spruce-tree gum and paraffin wax were popular in the United States until chicle was introduced in the late 1860s. What *is* new is the tooth-rotting capacity of all those sugary, synthetically minty, fruity, and spicy-flavored gums that have come along since the turn of the century.

If there is anything at all good that can be said about candy and chewing gum, it is that they don't pretend to be something they aren't—neither a nourishing breakfast cereal nor a healthful, thirst-quenching beverage. When you eat candy or chew gum, you *know* you're eating sugar and ingesting additives!

FROZEN MYSTERIES

Ice cream, on the other hand, is something of a frozen mystery. Sugar it has aplenty. In fact, that is one of the "all natural" ingredients that many ice-cream manufacturers actually boast about nowadays. But the cream, milk, and eggs used (if any) may be frozen or powdered rather than fresh, and even under the ice-cream labeling laws that went into effect in July 1979, the *form* of these ingredients does not have to be revealed.

The truth about coloring, too, is concealed; it may be artificial, and usually is, but the ice-cream label doesn't have to say so. (Sherbets and ices do have to tell if they are artificially colored. But you'd guess that anyhow from some of the hot pink, screaming orange, and jungle green colors they come in.)

The truth about the flavoring used in the ice cream *is* on the front of the carton, *if* you can read the code. "Vanilla-flavored" or "chocolate-flavored" means partly artificial and partly natural, with just slightly more of the natural flavoring. "Artificial" means mostly or all synthetic flavoring, while unmodified "vanilla" or "chocolate" is supposed to mean all natural flavoring.

As if the ice-cream labeling laws and commercial ingredients aren't confusing enough, there is also the question of the amount of air that has been whipped into the mixture. Federal law permits up to 50 percent air (by volume) in the scoop, pop, or carton of ice cream you buy. In ice-cream parlance, the air content is known as overrun. If there is as much air as there are ice-cream ingredients, a brand is said to have a 100 percent overrun.

The label won't give you the air content but you can sometimes tell there is a lot of air present by how fast an ice cream melts or by the presence of frothiness as tiny air bubbles come to the surface and burst. Ice creams without much air in them (low overrun) are usually richer-textured and denser. But an ice cream that melts slowly into a thickish soup isn't *necessarily* creamier; it may simply be more loaded up with thickeners and stabilizers like gelatin, or carrageenan, or a similar gum derived from seaweed or other plants.

Frozen bafflement indeed! You'll be saving calories by eating an ice cream that is half whipped air, but you may, in that case, find yourself eating more of it. Also, since not only the cheaper supermarket brands but a number of the more costly brands have high overruns, you may find yourself paying a premium price for entrapped air.

The home-made ice creams of the past had fewer and simpler ingredients and no artificial additives. Thomas Jefferson is credited with bringing ice cream to the White House in the early 1800s after he encountered it in France (although the original home of both ice cream and ices was sixteenth-century Italy). Ice cream soon became a fashionable dessert at official dinners hosted by Dolley Madison, the wife of Jefferson's presidential successor. The first commercial ice-cream maker was Baltimore-based Jacob Fussell in 1851. Half a century later, at the Louisiana Purchase Exposition of 1904 in St. Louis, the ice-cream cone was "invented" when a waffle was hastily rolled into a cone shape and pressed into service as an ice-cream holder.

Ice-cream parlors were popular gathering places during the first half of the twentieth century, before home freezers and commercially packaged ice cream became commonplace. Today's ice cream is mostly either fast food from quick stops like Baskin-Robbins, Carvel, or Dairy Queen, or home-freezer fare by Breyers, Sealtest (both products of Kraftco), or some other major food company. Along with added ingredients to achieve smoother textures or softer consistencies, have come flavors unheard of in the past— heavenly hash (chocolate, nuts, and marshmallow), cherry cheesecake, apple strudel, banana Daiquiri, and even such "sugar free" flavors as naturally sweet carob and honey ice creams.

Ice cream can be a fairly nutritious dessert rather than a junk food. But it would take a real labeling-law breakthrough to get manufacturers to tell all so that consumers could choose the better kinds and bypass those varieties that are high in sugar, air, and artificial ingredients.

POURING THE SALT

If processed foods have put more sugar in our lives, they have also increased our intake of salt (sodium chloride). As in the case of sugar, we are buying comparatively less salt in cartons at the store but we are eating more of it in the form of salted and smoked meats and fish, mustard, ketchup, pickles, olives, relishes, seasonings, bouillons, canned soups, frozen dinners, processed cheeses, peanut butter, and of course pretzels, popcorn, potato chips, and other salted snacks.

Processors also add salt to many nonsalty-tasting foods like canned and frozen vegetables, breads and cereals, and even to sweet products. At the same time many unprocessed foods like fresh meats and fish, natural cheeses, eggs, and milk are naturally high in sodium, a component of salt (table salt is 39 percent sodium and 61 percent chloride). So our intake can really soar.

Unlike the past, when salt was used mainly as a food preservative, processors today add it as a flavoring as well, and one that snack-oriented Americans have developed a very high tolerance for. Twenty salted french fries doused with two tablespoons of ketchup will supply half of the essential daily requirement of sodium. Yet many of us will also eat a cheeseburger or frankfurter, pickles, sauerkraut, and a host of perhaps less salty but nonetheless high-sodium foods in the course of the day. No wonder we get many times the amount of salt we ought to have.

With one in ten Americans believed to be suffering from persistent high blood pressure, or hypertension, the increasingly high consumption of salt among young people does not bode well for the future. An inborn tendency toward hypertension, combined with a too-salty diet, can bring on the disease itself, which can in later life lead to crippling strokes. High sodium intake is also related to heart disease and circulatory problems, and researchers report that a quantity of salted nuts or potato chips taken on an empty stomach may bring on severe migraine headaches in some individuals.

POPCORN TO PRINGLES

The challenge for snackers has always been to eat "just one salted peanut." Yet there is something hypnotizing about munching on any of the hundreds of oily, salty tidbits, ranging from popcorn to Pringles, that abound on the American snack scene.

Popcorn has its origin, of course, in the American past. The Incas of Peru knew about the small-seeded variety of corn that was good for popping. Its hard-husked kernels burst on heating because of the pressure built up by the moisture inside them. In the early 1600s, the Indians of the eastern seaboard introduced the first European colonists to popcorn.

But the Indian corn was unseasoned and bland-tasting, and it's doubtful that popcorn would have become so popular without the butter and salt that were subsequently added to it. In today's commercially prepared popcorn, however, saturated fat and artificial butter flavoring are often used instead of butter, and excessive salt may be added. So it's a good idea, whenever possible, to pop your own corn at home, adding real butter or an unsaturated fat, as preferred, and a reasonable amount of salt.

Fritos, Doritos, Chee-tos, and other corn chips in all their shapes and flavors also derive from Indian maize, for they are a modern snack version of the Mexican tortilla. The pancake-like tortilla, however, made from hulled, mashed corn kernels called masa, was also a bland food, while the crisply fried commercial tortilla chips are highly seasoned and heavily salted. Not surprisingly, most of the thirst-inducing corn chips marketed in the United States today are manufactured by Frito-Lay, a division of Pepsico, the company that makes Pepsi-Cola.

Pretzels, a salty snack based on wheat flour, reached American shores in the late 1600s with the arrival of the first wave of German settlers, called the Pennsylvania Dutch. Known as long ago as the time of the Crusades in Europe, and believed to represent a worshipper's arms crossed in prayer, pretzels—both crisp and soft varieties—were baked only in Pennsylvania farmhouse kitchens until the first commercial pretzel bakeries opened in that state in the mid-1800s.

Potato chips, on the other hand, were invented in nineteenth-century America. They have been in the snack repertory since 1853, when a chef in a hotel in Saratoga Springs, New York, created them to satisfy a guest who wanted his french fries sliced thinner. Saratoga chips was the name first given to these crisp, randomly curled slices.

Packaging has always been a problem for potato-chip manufacturers, for a single blow can pulverize the contents of an entire bagful. In the mid-1970s, Procter and Gamble launched Pringles, a premolded, stackable potato chip made with dehydrated potatoes, and sold in a hard-sided cylindrical container that resembled a tennis-ball can. Surprisingly, convenience packaging and massive advertising did not completely win over potato-chip lovers, for many rejected the uniform, factory-designed ovals put together with an extra dash of additives, and declared their loyalty to the more natural product made from whole fresh potatoes.

No matter how natural, however, it's important to recognize that high-salt snacks still rank as a potential health menace, and more so because they are designed to increase our intake of junk fluids, like sodas and other soft drinks, causing us to load up with excess sugar as well.

Fat is also a major ingredient in salted snacks. Potato chips, for example, are about 40 percent fat. The oil or other shortening is almost always the second most plentiful item after the corn, flour, peanuts, or potatoes—as those well-licked greasy fingers of ours will attest!

2 THE FAT OF THE LAND

Fats *are* fattening, no question about it, and one of the reasons is that a gram of fat yields 9 calories, while a gram of protein or carbohydrate yields only 4. Yet anyone who eats dairy or animal products—whole milk, butter, eggs, meat—is ingesting fat, and many vegetables, seeds, and nuts yield fat in the form of oils. Avoiding fats completely, even if one could, wouldn't be a good idea because the body requires fat. It is an important element in the composition of certain tissues, serves as skeletal padding, provides cushioning for internal organs, insulates against heat loss, and acts as stored energy. Fat is also an absorption medium for the fat-soluble vitamins, A, D, E, and K.

FAT FACTS

The main problems with fat are twofold. In a sedentary society like ours, many of us don't need as much fat as we're getting. Fats make up 42 percent of our total energy intake (compared to 12 percent from proteins and 46 percent from carbohydrates). The concentrated-calorie value of that fat-heavy portion of our diet is so great that unless we are woodchoppers or Olympic champions-in-training, the padding on hips, bellies, and elsewhere tends to build up, layer upon layer. It is estimated that 10 to 20 percent of American children and 35 to 50 percent of middle-aged

Americans are overweight, and about half of the latter group are likely to suffer serious, life-shortening illnesses as a result.

Being fat at any age can cause deep unhappiness because one's appearance is marred in a society that, despite its lavish and careless eating habits, idealizes the slim, youthful figure. But excess poundage, ranging all the way from plumpness to obesity, also contributes to heart disease, circulatory ailments, hernia, and gallbladder problems; and it increases the likelihood and the dangers of hypertension and diabetes.

Before the age of sixty, one in three men and one in six women in the United States have died of either heart disease or stroke. Excess fat intake is also believed to increase the incidence of breast and other cancers. Nutrition studies therefore recommend that we should reduce our average national fat intake from 42 percent of our total calories to about 30 percent, a paring down that won't be easy for Americans accustomed to rich eating.

The second major problem with the fat in our diet, we are told, is that there are good, bad, and indifferent *kinds* of fat, and we are all eating too much of the *wrong* kind—the saturated fats like butter, lard, beef fat, chicken fat, and certain vegetable oils like coconut and palm oil—as opposed to the unsaturated oils that are found in fish and in many vegetables and grains.

One way to tell the saturated fats is that they tend to become solid at room temperature, while unsaturated fats remain liquid. Chemically, a saturated or "bad" fat is one that has a full complement of hydrogen atoms on its fatty acid molecule. It cannot take on any more hydrogen, which is why we say it is saturated. Saturation gives it its stable, or solid, quality.

Safflower, sunflower, corn, soy, peanut, and other oils that do not solidify at room temperature are examples of unsaturated or "good" fats. The molecule of an unsaturated fat does have room for additional atoms of hydrogen. If the molecule has room for four or more hydrogen atoms, we say that the fat is polyunsaturated. If it has room for only two more hydrogen atoms, we call it a monounsaturated fat.

Polyunsaturated fats can become saturated fats through a laboratory process known as hydrogenation. In other words, the extra hydrogen atoms are added to the molecule so that the fat becomes solid. Some peanut butters are hydrogenated so that the oil won't separate from the peanut mash. Polyunsaturated oils are also hydrogenated to make solid baking fats like Crisco, and they are partially hydrogenated to make margarines that will remain solid at room temperature.

To find out why saturated fats are considered bad, we need to know what happens to them in the human body. A saturated fat tends to raise the level of cholesterol in the blood, a condition that can result in the deposit of cholesterol in the arteries, thickening their walls and partially clogging them. Known as atherosclerosis, this narrowing of the blood-supply passageways is one of the leading causes of heart disease. Polyunsaturates, on the other hand, are considered good fats because they appear to facilitate the excretion of cholesterol from the body, thus reducing its level in the blood stream. Monounsaturates seem to have no effect at all on the cholesterol in the body and so are rated neutral.

COUNTING CHOLESTEROL

What *is* cholesterol about which we've been hearing so much in recent years? Cholesterol is a waxy, alcoholic substance that is essential to certain body tissues and hormones. However, the body begins to manufacture its own cholesterol during the first year of life and from then on we really don't need much cholesterol, if any, in our diets.

Unfortunately, Americans and others, such as the Scandinavians, who eat a lot of animal and dairy products get a great deal of cholesterol in their diets. All animal fats—the bad-acting saturated fats—contain cholesterol, and it also occurs in lean, low-calorie animal organs like brains, kidneys, liver, and heart; in shrimp and lobster; and in egg yolk, which is the most widely eaten concentrated source.

It would seem then that the battle against too much cholesterol (both that which is manufactured by the body and that which we ingest) has to be fought on two fronts. First, many nutritionists tell us, we must reduce our intake of saturated fats and increase our intake of polyunsaturates. Second, we must try to reduce our cholesterol intake itself, from the current average of 600 milligrams a day to about 300 milligrams.

When we consider that the yolk of one egg contains 250 milligrams of cholesterol, we begin to understand why some studies advise that we eat no more than three eggs a week. The American breakfast of two fried-in-butter eggs with several strips of bacon, buttered toast, and coffee with cream is crammed with cholesterol. And suppose we follow it up with fried shrimp, a hamburger, or toasted cheese for lunch, and steak for dinner. Or perhaps a hearty main serving of surf-and-turf (steak and lobster tails)!

The cholesterol threat does seem to be a real one. Yet the experts have still not puzzled out the answers to certain questions of individual human response. Some people who eat a high-cholesterol diet show normal results on a cholesterol-count blood test. Other individuals, who try very hard to restrict the saturated fats and cholesterol in their diets, show a high count. It appears that some bodies manufacture more cholesterol on their own, which then courses around at a high level in the blood stream, while others seem to excrete both body-manufactured and dietary cholesterol more efficiently.

Trying to avoid an excess of saturated fats *and* cholesterol is a real challenge. Some people turn to processed foods like nondairy coffee creamers, margarine, and whipped toppings. But these substitutes are frequently not the answer. Powdered, liquid, or frozen coffee lighteners often contain highly saturated palm oil or coconut oil plus a host of additives, and the same is true for imitation whipped cream. A sample label from one such frozen dessert topping reads: "water, vegetable shortening, sugar, dextrose, sodium caseinate, polysorbate 60, hexaglycerol distearate, vegetable gums, pure and imitation flavor, carrageenan, artificial color." The additives sound intimidating enough. But what we aren't told is the *kind* of vegetable shortening, and therefore we don't know whether it is a saturated or unsaturated type. The imitation topping may well contain more saturated fat than real whipped cream!

Margarine, to be considered at all as a butter substitute, should be made with vegetable oils of low saturation and never with animal fats such as lard or beef fat. The label should indicate more "liquid" oil (listed first) than "partially hydrogenated" oil, and the label should also tell you whether the oil is safflower, sunflower, corn, soybean, or cottonseed. These oils range, in descending order, from about 75 percent to 50 percent in polyunsaturate content. Some people, however, avoid cottonseed oil completely because cotton is not grown primarily as a food crop and is sprayed with strong pesticides.

Olive oil, which is too costly to be found in margarines, is very high in monounsaturates and therefore neutral in its effect on cholesterol in the body. Sesame and peanut oils, which contain substantial amounts of both mono- and polyunsaturates, are also relatively low in saturated fat.

BUTTER VERSUS MARGARINE

Americans have been using margarine for over a century, ever since its introduction from France in 1874. Like several other processed foods developed in the nineteenth century, margarine was a wartime invention, born of the Franco-Prussian War of 1870, when butter became scarce. The French chemist, Hippolyte Mege-Mouries, who devised this butter substitute, combined beef fat, milk, water, and a yellow vegetable dye from the berry of the tropical annatto tree. The animal fat, which was called "oleo oil," plus the word margarine from the Greek for pearl (indicating shininess) were combined to give it the name oleomargarine at first.

The butter-versus-margarine controversy has been raging since the latter's invention, and has peaked since the discovery of the possible nutritional dangers of saturated fat. Should you substitute a good quality margarine (high in polyunsaturates) for butter? Natural-food purists say no because of the artificial flavorings, colorings, emulsifiers, preservatives, and other additives in margarine. However, butter too is treated with additives, particularly when it is made from cream that has soured, and it is often artificially colored. But, because of the strong lobbying influence of the dairy industry, the label doesn't have to say so. Margarine labels, on the other hand, have to be quite explicit.

The report of the U.S. Senate Select Committee on Nutrition and Human Needs favors the use of margarine over butter. In view of the high cost plus the high saturated-fat content of butter, and because of the advertising health claims of the margarine manufacturers, many Americans have switched, so that margarine now outsells butter at least two to one. Yet there is no question that butter, provided it is fresh and of good quality, is superior in flavor. Probably the best approach is to use butter in those dishes and baked goods where flavor is most important and, in general, to learn to spread it thinner. As butter and margarine are equally high in fat content, there is no difference in the number of calories they supply—a little over 1,600 each per pound.

HIDDEN FAT

Since fat, like sugar and salt, adds a tastiness to food, to which our conditioned palates respond eagerly, food processors don't hesitate to use substantial amounts of shortening in snack foods, crackers, baked goods, cake mixes, and other products. Yet their labels don't tell us the whole story for, when "vegetable fats" or "vegetable oils" are listed, the kind of fat is not always revealed. Where labels are more explicit, careful reading will often turn up the presence of saturated fats like coconut or palm oil, or of animal fats such as beef fat or lard, all of which it is probably better to avoid.

Fat is "sneaked" into our food in other ways. Cattlemen "finish" beef animals by feeding them costly grain for a marbling, or distribution, of fat in the meat, which increases tenderness and flavor. And poultry producers, trying to pare the costs of "finishing," inject turkeys with additional fat *after* slaughtering to make them tastier. But the "self-basting" mixture inserted under the skin of the dressed bird is usually a blend of coconut oil, water, and artificial butter flavoring. The widely marketed Swift's Butterball turkey, for example, has no butter in it. Processing, in this case, is not only misleading but imposes on us a turkey with a lacing of saturated fat and additives that we may not want.

Similarly, many frozen dinners and other precooked supermarket items, and the fries, shakes, doughnuts, and other specialties of the fast food chains are very high in fat content. We almost never know what kind of fat has been used, and all too often it is one of the cheaper saturated types.

It is only by bypassing processed foods and choosing whole foods—foods that are as close to natural as possible—that we can gain control of what we eat, and cut down on the fat in our diets. Eating whole foods can also help us to avoid excess sugar and salt, as well as the many synthetic additives of questionable safety that the food technologists and the food companies have been heaping onto our dinner plates for years.

3 ADDING UP THE ADDITIVES

"Additive," "artificial," and "chemical" have all become dirty words in late twentieth-century America. The laboratory discoveries of the past, such as that of saccharin, were once hailed as beneficial, but are now seen as detrimental. And time has revealed to us the dangers of a number of synthetic substances added to our food in recent decades.

Among these have been cyclamates, the sugar substitute that was banned from sale in 1970; DES (diethylstilbestrol), a synthetic female hormone added to cattle and sheep feeds to stimulate and speed growth, temporarily banned because of high residues in 1973 (but returned to use in 1974); and the coloring agents Red No. 2 and Red No. 4, banned in 1976. All were linked to cancer and/or birth abnormalities.

Synthetic additives in our food go all the way back to the mid-1800s when the first food colorings derived from coal-tar oil appeared. Soon these dyes, which were highly toxic, were being used to brightly color candies designed to attract children. But it wasn't until 1906 that the first federal food laws were passed. Government action was spurred, in part, by the tainted beef sold during the Spanish-American War and the scandalous conditions in the meat-packing industry. Impure, adulterated, and harmful food products continued to proliferate, however, and the more forceful Food, Drug, and Cosmetic Act was passed in 1938 to combat such public hoaxes as a "raspberry jam" that consisted of a red-dyed gelatinous sugar mixture containing hayseeds!

Today there are approximately 3,000 additives on the market, causing overwhelming confusion not only to the consumer but to the FDA (Food and Drug Administration), the federal agency that is responsible for authorizing, or prohibiting, their use. Additives that have been introduced *since 1958* (the date of the Food Additives Amendment) are supposed to have been adequately tested first by their sponsors and the test results approved by the FDA before they can be put into use. But those on the market *before* that cut-off date were not pretested and were lumped by the FDA into a gray category labeled GRAS ("generally recognized as safe") to await testing at a later date. Of the six hundred or so pre-1958 additives, only about half have been reviewed so far. Most have been declared safe. But not all.

Testing additives is a tricky and uncertain business, mainly because long-term effects and the interaction of additives with each other and with substances in the human body cannot really be determined in laboratory experiments. That is why more and more people feel that the safest course is to avoid additive-laden foods as much as possible, even those containing "safe" ones.

NATURAL VERSUS ARTIFICIAL

What *is* a safe additive? Is it a *natural* substance like molasses extract (from sugar), which is used for coloring, or gelatin (from bones), which is used for thickening? These natural additives do seem totally safe. But there are also natural substances, like caffeine and quinine, that are considered harmful. Caffeine causes hyperactivity and jitteriness, and both these plant derivatives are suspected links to birth defects. Gum tragacanth, a plant-derived thickener and stabilizer used in salad dressings and other viscous foods, can cause allergic reactions such as swollen tissues and serious breathing impairment in some individuals. And substances like sugar, salt, pepper, mustard, and other spices, herbs, and extracts are widely used natural additives—some of which may be harmful if taken in excess, as so frequently are sugar and salt.

Another thing to remember is that many additives that come from natural sources, such as vegetable gums, milk casein, and hydrolyzed vegetable protein (HVP) are treated with "artificial" laboratory compounds in the process of their derivation.

So we can't always separate natural from artificial, nor can we say that natural is always "good" while synthetic is always "bad." We all know that spoiled food, resulting from the *natural* growth of bacteria, yeasts, and fungi, can cause severe food poisoning and even death. Certain synthetic food additives have reduced these risks drastically. Sodium benzoate, for example, is a food preservative that has been in use for nearly a century to keep microorganisms from growing in pickles, preserves, fruit juices, and carbonated drinks. Calcium propionate, another synthetic preservative in long use, keeps fungus molds from growing on bread and other baked goods.

As very few Americans are able to feed themselves a total diet of fresh foods nearly every day, additives like these will almost certainly continue to be part of our food supply. However, until we know much more about them than we do now, we should be aware that their use does involve a trade-off. Some of us may want to avoid benzoated sodas and to bake and freeze our own bread as often as possible. Individual choices will have to be made by weighing the convenience benefits of processed foods against the possible health risks.

Known health risks *are* involved in the consumption of the synthetic additives—sodium *nitrate* and sodium *nitrite*—that are used to preserve cured meats and fish, including frankfurters, bologna, salami, corned beef, bacon, and ham. Nitrates and nitrites retard spoilage and inhibit the growth of deadly botulism bacteria. They also give these foods the red coloring and the flavoring to which we are accustomed.

However, once in the stomach, nitrates and nitrites are converted into substances called nitrosamines, which cause cancer in laboratory animals and are believed to cause cancer in humans. Bacon is considered especially risky because nitrosamines can form during the high-heat cooking period, increasing their concentration in the body.

Today's frankfurter-loving public is faced with a dilemma. If the FDA eventually decides to ban nitrates and nitrites, the food industry will probably be forced to come up with a satisfactory-tasting and eye-appealing alternative that might also be safer. But industry pressures against major and costly changes in food processing are strong. And, meantime, consumers who want preservative-free hot dogs and other processed meats will have to settle for brownish links, slabs, and slices that are sold mainly from the freezer cases of health food stores, at prices that far exceed the standard commercial product. Nor do the flavors of the nitrite-free meats generally measure up to expectation.

In view of the accompanying high-fat and high-salt content of cured meats, it's probably wisest to drastically reduce our consumption of them, or avoid them totally, pending FDA action on the nitrate/nitrite issue.

Synthetic additives are, of course, put into processed foods for purposes other than to prevent spoilage, to add coloring, or to provide flavoring. They act as leavening agents (baking soda, baking powder); bleaching agents (to whiten flour); thickeners, stabilizers, and emulsifiers (to improve texture and keep ingredients evenly distributed) as in candies, baked goods, margarine, frozen desserts, and peanut butter.

In addition, laboratory-synthesized vitamins and minerals are added to white bread, cornmeal, rice, and macaroni for enrichment and fortification—in other words, to supply nutrients that have either been lost in processing or that never existed in these widely eaten grains.

Some purists reject the B vitamins, iron, calcium, and vitamins A and D added to so many cereal and dairy products, and the potassium iodide added to table salt—often by law—because they are synthetic rather than natural substances. But most scientists tell us that the two are chemically identical and that there is no difference in our body's response to them, for all food elements found in nature are themselves composed of chemicals. And some of these elements *can* be successfully synthesized in the laboratory.

DECEPTIVE OR WORSE

The real problem with "fortification" additives like synthetic vitamins and minerals is that the food industry passes off artificial fruit drinks, sugary breakfast cereals, packaged cupcakes, and other junk foods as "highly nutritious" because they have been "enriched." It would be far better to get one's vitamins, plus many other nutrients *not* present in junk foods, from pure fruit juices, whole grains, and fresh fruits.

Additives also make other deceptions possible, as when food is artificially colored or flavored, or made to seem creamy or fluffy with gums and emulsifiers rather than with cream or egg whites. Cheap ingredients can thus be substituted for more expensive ones for the profit of the processed-food manufacturer.

It is far more serious, however, when the food industry goes beyond mere deception into potentially harmful practices. In addition to sodium nitrates and nitrites (which *are* required by law to be listed on labels), food colorings are highly suspect among today's synthetic additives. Although they are widely used in candies, beverages, gelatin and pudding mixes, processed fruit desserts, ices and sherbets, baked goods, and other heavily consumed foods of low nutritional value, the label seldom tells us the name of the dye that has been used as "artificial coloring."

While dyes like Red No. 2 and Red No. 4 have been banned, several suspicious dyes are still in use, among them Red No. 40, which is believed carcinogenic to animals, and Yellow No. 5, which is allergenic to humans. Until food processors offer specific information voluntarily, or are required to do so by law, we would probably do best to give a wide berth to all foods containing artificial coloring, even though their colors are listed as "U.S. Certified," just as Red No. 2 and Red No. 4 once were.

Also high on the current enemies list of additives are BHT (butylated hydroxytoluene) and BHA (butylated hydroxyanisole). Both are used as antioxidants, to prevent rancidity in fat-containing products like potato chips, corn chips, and salad oils. They are also used to maintain "freshness" and extend shelf life in dry cereals, cake mixes, chewing gums, and candies. BHT is believed to be cancer-causing and allergenic; BHA is considered only slightly safer. Both, however, continue to be widely used pending further study by the FDA.

Another junk food additive that is under suspicion but has not been banned is BVO (brominated vegetable oil). BVO is an emulsifier that is often used in citrus-flavored soft drinks to keep the cloudy citrus portion dispersed throughout the liquid. This additive leaves a residue that has poisonous properties and can be stored in body tissues. Like BHT and BHA, BVO is relatively easy to avoid by cutting down on our junk food intake.

An additive that is not so easy to avoid is MSG (monosodium glutamate), for it is a popular flavor enhancer that occurs naturally in seaweed, soybeans, and sugar beets. It has long been used in the Orient, and became commercially popular in the United States in the early 1900s. MSG is included in most factory-prepared soups, sauces, stews, and seasoning mixtures, and it can make meat and poultry dishes taste more "beefy" or "chickeny" than they really are. Its widespread use in Chinese restaurants has identified it as the cause of "Chinese Restaurant Syndrome," dizziness and/or headache combined with tightness or numbness in the head, neck, chest, and arms, which comes on shortly after eating.

Adults generally throw off the symptoms in an hour or two with no known aftereffects, but the discovery some years ago that MSG damaged brain cells in baby mice brought an angry public outcry that halted its use in jarred baby foods in 1969. However, as MSG is still on the GRAS list, it is present in many foods that babies and young children do eat. And there are even some foods—like mayonnaise and salad dressings—that can contain MSG without a federal requirement that this additive be listed on the label.

ADDITIVES IN WHOLE FOODS

Processed foods and restaurant fare are surely the chief culprits where additives in our snacks and meals are concerned. But sadly, even whole foods, the refuge of the additive-weary, have been tampered with by growers and raisers, packers and distributors on their journey from seedpod to supermarket.

When the pesticide DDT came into use in the 1940s, it was hailed as a miracle compound that would vastly decrease crop losses from insect damage. It was, if anything, too effective. By the time its hazards were recognized and controls were instituted, it had built up residues in soil, water, plants, animals, and humans. Traces of DDT and other pesticides in our food and in our bodies will probably be with us for a long time to come. Similarly, industrial chemicals called PCBs (polychlorinated biphenyls) have invaded our environment, affecting plant life and even sea life, and leaving small toxic deposits in animal and human body fat and other tissues.

In addition to these widespread contaminants that have seeped into our food supply over the years, produce growers continue to use pesticides, fungicides, herbicides, and synthetic fertilizers that have not been tested for long-term effects. And livestock raisers medicate their poultry and cattle with antibiotics and tranquilizers for maximum meat production. Residues of these chemicals tend to concentrate in the fatty tissues and livers of the animals to which they are fed, and are then passed on in small but cumulative amounts to meat-eating humans.

Other synthetic chemicals added to whole foods are the gases, dyes, and waxes used on fruits and vegetables to make them attractive to the consumer, who has been conditioned to seeing glossy and vivid-hued food, as reproduced in magazines and on the TV screen. We've all known for years that most store tomatoes have usually been picked in some faraway place and artificially reddened en route by spraying them with ethylene gas. The hard, unripe tomatoes hold up well to their long freight-car journeys and look rosy at market, but they never have the flavor of vine-ripened tomatoes. Nor do they have as much vitamin C.

Similarly, some green-skinned Florida oranges are artificially colored orange with a dye called Citrus Red No. 2, which is a suspected carcinogen. Although the dye does not seep through into the pulp, some consumers use orange rind in marmalade, baking, or other cooking, or simply like to nibble on it raw. As a result of industry objections, dyed oranges no longer need to be stamped "color added."

Food dyes may color our "unprocessed" poultry supply, too. That healthy-looking, golden-skinned, golden-fleshed chicken from the supermarket may very well have been raised on chicken feed that has had yellow pigments added to it.

The term "waxed fruit" sounds disturbingly similar to "wax fruit," those inedible imitation apples, bananas, and bunches of grapes that once decorated old-fashioned dining-room sideboards. But waxed fruit is *real* fruit— apples, pears, plums, oranges, melons—and also vegetables like tomatoes, green peppers, cucumbers, potatoes, carrots, squash, eggplants, and others that have been sprayed by produce packers with a thin-to-moderately-thick coating of wax in order to add luster, reduce bruising, and retard shriveling.

Some fruits and vegetables are customarily peeled before eating. But what about those that are not? The wax-coating on an apple, for example, is difficult to see and impossible to wash off completely, but it does show up easily when the skin is lightly scraped with a sharp knife. Although the wax itself *may* be harmless, its application may have entrapped some of the pesticide with which the fruit or vegetable was sprayed before picking. So here is another industry-imposed additive that certainly does not benefit the consumer.

LABELING LAPSES

"Unprocessed," or whole foods, very seldom carry labels that tell us about the gases, dyes, waxes, and other spoilage retardants and cosmetic embellishments that have been added to them, for in most cases such labeling is not required by law at the point of retail sale. We may also wonder why certain *processed* foods like mayonnaise, ketchup, salad dressings, noodles and macaroni, and some canned fruit and vegetable products do not list all their ingredients on their labels.

The reason is that they presumably conform to the FDA's "standard of identity" for that product. In other words, if a jar of mayonnaise contains a certain amount of vegetable oil, plus lemon juice or vinegar, and egg yolks, it can be labeled simply "mayonnaise" (even though MSG may be among its flavoring ingredients along with the sugar, salt, and spices). In recent years, however, the proliferation of substitute ingredients and additives has spurred a movement to take some processed foods out of this category. Ice cream lost its "standard of identity" status in July 1979, after which date manufacturers were required to list all ingredients on the label (with the exception of artificial coloring, a concession made by the government to the powerful dairy industry).

Labeling lapses extend to wine and beer, which are no longer the natural beverages that once they were. Numerous synthetic chemicals are used in wine- and beer-making today. While the French government permits 27 additives in wine, American winemakers are allowed about 70, in addition to sulfur dioxide, which is universally used and was known even in ancient Roman times. Sulfur dioxide acts as a sterilizing agent, to kill unwanted yeasts and enzymes, and to prevent the wine from turning into vinegar.

Beer, too, contains some 60 federally approved chemical agents of both natural and synthetic derivation, including a preservative called heptyl-para-hydroxy-benzoate, or heptyl paraben for short. Are these additives safe? No one really knows. As many people smoke while they drink alcohol, or drink in a smoke-filled atmosphere, there is the possibility of a harmful interaction between cigarette smoke and alcohol, or among these two plus certain proteins in the body. Such an interaction might have carcinogenic effects.

At present the U.S. Treasury Department's Bureau of Alcohol, Tobacco, and Firearms—the agency responsible for alcoholic-beverage labeling—does not require wine and beer labels to list any additives. Needless to say, the wine and beer industries strongly oppose such labeling.

FDA LAG

Coke-drinking children running rampant on caffeine highs; woozy adults with Chinese Restaurant Syndrome; breakfast bacon sizzling with cancer-causing nitrosamines; potato chips with BHT; soda pop with BVO; orange skins dyed with dangerous artificial coloring; and supposedly edible apples coated with wax—we must ask why all these potentially harmful additives and unsound practices haven't been banned by our government.

The answer is complex. The FDA is responsible for the safety of drugs and cosmetics as well as foods. It moves slowly in its elephantine task of regulation and is tangled in masses of bureaucratic red tape. In addition, it is pressured by powerful food- and drug-company lobbyists to delay or reconsider changes that would lead to business losses. Often, in the past, the agency has been headed by officials who themselves had ties to the food industry.

Even though the FDA was empowered by the Delaney clause, which was part of the Food Additives Amendment of 1958, to ban any food substances proven to cause cancer in laboratory animals, test results have frequently been challenged as inconclusive. The validity of the Delaney clause has been challenged, too, based on the fact that some scientists say they do not know for sure whether substances that cause cancer in animals do so in humans.

Representatives of the food and chemical industries also argue that animals are often fed high concentrations of additives that humans would be unlikely to duplicate in their own diets. Lastly, the public itself has sometimes appeared to be its own worst enemy, as in its outcry against the banning of saccharin. All of these pressures make the FDA slow to act.

Many additives in use today are unnecessary and others could have their concentrations reduced for greater safety. Some are so threatening that they should be banned and safer substitutes should be found.* Meantime, the consumer is caught between a $160 billion food industry that is not above sloppily pretesting, or even rigging, test results on an additive that it wants badly to market, and a lumbering government agency. Often the public must wait years for the results of FDA reviews and decisions on hazardous substances that have been removed from the GRAS list but not from the food supply.

What can you and I do? We can try to avoid additive-laden processed foods as much as possible. Whole, or unprocessed, foods are still a better choice, especially those that have the shortest distance to travel from farm to market and the fewest intermediate agents between farmer and consumer. In-season fruits and vegetables from farmstands, and products from local egg and dairy farms are preferable, if we have access to them.

Farmers' markets have recently become popular in American cities, both large and small, because their produce, although not usually organically grown, is generally fresher than that in the supermarket and less likely to be gassed, dyed, or waxed. Organically grown and raised food is a good choice, too, but *only* if it is fresh, of good quality, and from a reliable source, so that you can be certain it was produced without chemicals, is wholesome, and worth the higher cost.

Sugar, salt, fats, and additives—these are the main ingredients of most junk foods and nutritionally borderline fare that Americans eat today. Yet even though most of us are indignant about food-industry abuses and government

---

*A list of common food additives with their uses, applications, and known or suspected health risks will be found in the Appendix.

inaction, we are all too likely to saunter into the next fast-food restaurant for a burger, fries, and a Coke.

American families now spend between one-third and one-half of their food dollars on meals away from home, for they are attracted to the quick-service convenience of today's restaurant chains. But eating meals out—whether they are school lunches, fast-food snacks, or sit-down dinners—is, as we'll see, hardly the route to a healthier diet.

THE FAST-FOOD PHENOMENON

Americans have been described as a people who are always "on the move." Speed that up a little to "on the run," and you can easily see why fast food has become a way of life for most of us.

The railroads pioneered eating-on-the-move way back in the mid-1800s when the very first dining cars appeared, featuring one long center table that ran the length of the car. Before the building of the railways, travelers had always interrupted their journeys for meals. The passengers of horse-drawn coaches stopped at wayside inns; covered-wagon trains halted at "nooning" time and at suppertime. The wagons were then drawn into a protective circle against attack, a sort of corral inside which families would start the cookfires for their meals.

In 1868 George Mortimer Pullman, who had developed the railway sleeping car with convertible berths a few years earlier, put the first luxurious dining car on the tracks. Small tables with crisp white-linen tablecloths and gleaming china and cutlery were arranged on both sides of a center aisle, each table with a window view of the passing scenery. The kitchen was located at the end of the car, or in the next car, and brisk, uniformed waiters served freshly cooked hot meals, comparable to those in the finest restaurants.

But dinner in the diner (like a berth in the sleeping car)

was not for everybody. Poorer travelers grabbed a bite at the informal and often dreary quick-lunch counters in the railway stations, or brought along a box lunch to eat in their seats. The Pullman dining car had such an attractive image, though, and was so expressive of the mobile efficiency of the sleek new America, that a couple of decades later stationary restaurants shaped like railway cars began to appear in cities and towns, and were called diners. These eateries combined the quick-lunch counter, with its row of high stools, or with individual tables or booths where the service was guaranteed to be almost equally fast. Americans fell in love with the casual, informal diner, where you could have a cup of coffee or an entire meal at almost any hour of the day or night.

As rail travel began to decline and auto highways took over during the first half of the twentieth century, roadside diners sprang up. Along with smaller "mom and pop" eateries that were sometimes extensions of wayside farmhouses, they became favorite stopping places for truckers, traveling salesmen, and families on outings.

THE AUTOMATED CAFETERIA

Another informal type of eatery that had been around since the 1800s was the cafeteria, a self-service restaurant where you picked up your food at a counter and took it to a table or to a tall "stand-up" counter to eat. Near the turn of the century, a new twist on the cafeteria appeared in the cities of Philadelphia and New York—the Automat. The very name given to this revolutionary chain of restaurants, run by the Horn & Hardart Company, told you that they were part of the marvelous new age of automation.

As soon as you entered one of the large, gleaming Automats, you headed straight for the change booth to have your quarters and half-dollars converted into nickels. Even the cashier at the Automat was an automaton-like marvel of speed and efficiency. Next you made the rounds of dozens of little glass-door compartments, set in rows along the walls, behind which waited sandwiches, baked beans, macaroni-and-cheese, salads, rolls, cakes, and pies. If you wanted a ham sandwich, you dropped three or four nickles into the slot according to the printed instructions, the glass door popped open, you lifted the lid, took out your order, and carried it to a vacant place at one of the tables. Hot and cold drinks came out of spigots under which you set your glass or cup. And there was also a counter-service steam table for hot meats and vegetables, as in the conventional cafeteria.

Automat food was in the genteel American tradition that had been established by Fanny Farmer, in revolt against the coarse, heavy, greasy meals of frontier America. Daintily filled white-bread sandwiches, creamed dishes, orange-iced cupcakes, and apple pie gently bathed in warm vanilla sauce were among the mainstays. Only the New England-style baked beans served in individual earthenware bean pots and the crisp, raisiny honey buns, reminiscent of German-inspired Philadelphia sticky buns, seemed to have genuine regional or ethnic roots.

No matter! People from eight to eighty adored the Automats, even if one did have to share tables with strangers at crowded hours. Depending on the neighborhoods in which they were located, the Automats were frequented at various times of the day by secretaries, salesmen, gamblers, theater folk, clusters of students, and solitary older people. Some stayed just long enough for a bun and a cup of coffee, but others lingered at the tables for hours. Depression-era businessmen of the 1930s were said to maintain "offices" at the local Automat, and indeed, order books and sample cases were often in evidence.

In the long run, however, rising costs and table-hogging patrons cut into profits; American tastes changed, newer and faster eateries appeared, and the Automats began to close one by one. Today only one or two samples of these "period-piece" restaurants remain.

HOT DOGS AND HAMBURGERS

The hot dog and the hamburger did a lot to set the stage for the fast food restaurants of today. German immigrants of the nineteenth century brought the first wieners and Hamburg steak to the United States. Traditionally, these foods were served on a plate, accompanied by sauerkraut, potatoes, or some other vegetable, and eaten with a knife and fork. Bread was served on the side.

Sometime around the turn of the century, however, franks and burgers were put onto buns, slathered with mustard and sauerkraut or pickles and ketchup, and became "finger foods." A Coney Island, New York, beer-garden-owner named Charles Feltman is credited with putting the first frankfurter on an elongated soft roll. No one is completely certain when the first hamburger was fitted between a sliced round bun, but by 1904 you could buy one of these juicy hot sandwiches at the St. Louis world's fair, officially called the Louisiana Purchase Exposition because it commemorated (a year late) the hundredth-anniversary of that event.

The really fast food frankfurter leaped to national fame in 1916 with the opening of a bustling hot dog and soft-drink stand in Coney Island known as Nathan's. The owner,

Nathan Handwerker, had formerly worked at the far-more-fashionable Feltman beer garden. The going price for a frankfurter on a roll was ten cents, but at Nathan's, hot dogs sold for only a nickel and were made from a secret blend of beef and spices worked out by Mrs. Handwerker. Customers soon flocked to the new sidewalk eatery, just a stone's throw from the beachfront. On warm summer evenings, people stood twelve deep at the outdoor counter calling out their orders. And halfway across the country, in the Midwest and in the Southwest, hot dogs on buns soon got to be known as "Coney Islands."

But there was something daring and even a little dangerous about eating chopped- or ground-meat concoctions offered by casual vendors, foodsellers that didn't have an established reputation. What was inside those patties and links? There were rumors that hot dogs contained other things besides beef or pork muscle, that they were catchalls for the ears, snouts, lips, lungs, diaphragms, hearts, skin, and blood vessels of animals that included sheep, goats, and chickens, as well as cattle and hogs. And those rumors happened to be true. In addition, the public had already been alerted to the nation's filthy slaughtering-house conditions in Upton Sinclair's muckraking book, *The Jungle*, published in 1906.

Even after federal food laws got into the act, the government approved the use of certain meat organs and other parts plus, in 1924, the use of the chemicals, sodium nitrate and sodium nitrite in cured meats. The U.S. Department of Agriculture regulations also were to allow up to 30 percent fat, 10 percent water, and 5 percent spices, flavorings, colorings, and preservatives, so that even frankfurters that were advertised as "all beef" or "all meat" could actually be 45 percent nonmeat!

Other types of frankfurters were permitted to contain cereal, milk solids, and other extenders as well, and therefore even less meat. Federal inspection was supposed to guarantee the cleanliness of the hot dog factories and the wholesomeness of their frankfurters, but who could be sure of what really got into the grinding machines when nobody was looking?

Maybe it was the public's growing suspicions about the hot dog stand product that led to the frankfurter's being outranked in popularity by the hamburger by the 1930s. The cheeseburger appeared about that time, too—a slice of processed cheese melted atop a sizzling meat patty— offering a variation that caught the public's fancy.

But even the less complicated hamburger was believed to be a risky buy (fatty, subject to rapid spoilage, easily contaminated with bacteria due to unclean handling, even infested with insect fragments and rodent hairs) unless it came from a major chain such as White Castle. The turreted White Castle hamburger shops first appeared in 1921 and were modeled after the Chicago water tower, which was supposed to be a symbol of purity and strength. Along with its thin 2½-inch-square burgers, the chain sold the idea of wholesomeness and dependability, and so gained a share of the public's trust.

MASS-PRODUCED FAST FOOD

More and more, the idea of reliability through standardization was selling twentieth-century Americans on big-name companies and chain-store marketing, whether they were buying A&P groceries, Walgreen drugs, or Woolworth dry goods. And by the time World War II had ended, in 1945, soldiers had gotten accustomed to mess-hall food and C rations, and defense-factory workers had become acquainted with the institutionalized fare that was served in company canteens and cafeterias. Such mass-produced food didn't taste like homemade (which was sometimes wonderful and sometimes not), but it fed large numbers of people quickly and it was considered hygienic and safe.

By 1955, when the first McDonald's was opened in Des Plaines, Illinois, by an enterprising milkshake-machine salesman named Ray Kroc, Americans had already gotten their first taste of mass-produced postwar foods like TV dinners and airline meals. What McDonald's offered was a cheap, fast, sanitary meal put together out of prefabricated parts in assembly-line fashion. And, as the chain rapidly expanded, it added the reassurance of a coast-to-coast name and a hamburger guaranteed to look and taste exactly the same whether it was eaten in Allentown or in Albuquerque.

You could be sure there'd be no variation because a McDonald basic-type pure beef hamburger, before cooking, was precisely .221 inches thick, 3.875 inches in diameter, and weighed 1.6 ounces. Rigid measurement and quality standards also applied to the buns, pickle slices, french fries, shake ingredients, and to the fish-filet sandwiches, apple pie, ice-cream sundaes, Egg McMuffins, and other items that were added to the menu during the 1960s and 1970s.

Through a system known as franchising, McDonald's and other fast food outfits were soon able to blanket the United States in company-chosen locations, just the way the nationwide motel chains and the big oil-corporation gas stations had done. Soon many of the fast food branches were not company-run but were operated by individual owners who franchised, or licensed, the right to use the chain name and all of its identifying paraphernalia. The franchisees were supposed to conform, however, in every detail to the company formula. McDonald's made sure of this by sending its owner-licensees to its Hamburger University in Elk Grove, Illinois, for a fast-paced management course that earned them a "Bachelor of Hamburgerology" degree.

Today, however, some of the fast food companies are cutting back on franchises and taking direct control of more of their branches. They've learned that one rusty link— caused by a licensee who's careless about cleanliness, service, or food quality—can damage the entire chain.

One thing a fast food shop manager or owner-licensee doesn't have to worry about is hiring and keeping a good cook. Teenage part-timers can handle all the cooking that's necessary, for the operation is so automated and so streamlined that all one has to do is respond to the bells, buzzers, and other timing devices that tell when the preshaped hamburger is done, when the precooked fries are hot, and when the shake is whipped to the proper icy thickness.

To no one's surprise, the fast food success formula soon spawned scores of competing hamburger chains, to say nothing of fried chicken, fish-and-chips, pizza, pancake, taco, doughnut, and ice-cream outfits. The "mom and pop" eateries, individually owned coffee shops, and even large roadside diners were squeezed out in favor of the well-advertised, fast-turnover, uniform product offered by the new giants of the highways.

Soon cities, towns, and suburban areas were infiltrated, too. Tea rooms and lunchrooms that had once served home-baked pies and pastries, homemade soups and breads, vanished almost overnight. No one seemed to mind that fast food meant a limited menu, that it lacked variety of taste, that the adventure had gone out of American eating. Nor did anyone mind that children raised on stamped-out hamburgers and cardboard pizzas would be unlikely to recognize the taste of spontaneously prepared good food, or be able to appreciate a fine gastronomic experience if they should ever stumble upon one.

For folksy and family-run as some of the names of the fast food chains sound, all are owned or operated by huge, impersonal organizations. Colonel Sanders' Kentucky Fried Chicken is owned by Heublein, the food and alcoholic beverage conglomerate that also gives us Smirnoff vodka, Italian Swiss Colony wines, and A-1 Steak Sauce. Stuckey's is owned by Pet, purveyors of canned milk, cereals, applesauce, and Old El Paso Mexican products. Ralston Purina, the huge animal-feed manufacturer, and Pillsbury, the flour-milling giant, give us Jack-in-the-Box and Burger King, respectively. Burger Chef is owned by General Foods, Pizza Hut by Pepsico, and Arby's by Royal Crown Cola. Big-business takeovers of successful chains are increasingly common, for over one-third of all the restaurant business done in the United States today is in the booming fast food sector.

Battles rage, though, even among the giants. Out front in the hamburger supremacy race is McDonald's with 20 percent of the market. In 1979, Burger King held second place with 8 percent, and Wendy's, a fast-growing Ohio-based chain, was in third place with 2 percent. Concern about rising beef prices, reduced auto travel due to gasoline shortages and rising gasoline prices, and market saturation keeps both the bigger and smaller chains on their toes. All are anxious to have the teenagers, young families, school-lunch crowds, and other fast food customers continue to patronize their establishments.

THE EATING-OUT SOCIETY

What makes Americans spend nearly half their food dollars on meals away from home? The answers lie in the way Americans live today. During the first few decades of the twentieth century, canned and other convenience foods freed the family cook from full-time duty at the kitchen range. Then, in the 1940s, work in the wartime defense plants took more women out of the home than ever before, setting the pattern of the working wife and mother.

Today about half of the country's married women are employed outside the home. But, unless family members pitch in with food preparation, women are not fully liberated from that chore. Instead many have become, in a sense, prisoners of the completely cooked convenience meal. It's easier to pick up a bucket of fried chicken on the way home from work or take the family out for pizzas, heroes, or burgers than to start opening cans or heating up frozen dinners after a long, hard day.

Also, the rising divorce rate means that there are more single working parents with children to feed. And many young adults and elderly people, as well as unmarried and divorced mature people, live alone rather than as part of a family unit and don't want to bother cooking for one.

Fast food is appealing because it *is* fast, it doesn't require any dressing up, it offers a "fun" break in the daily routine, and the outlay of money seems small. It can be eaten in the car—sometimes picked up at a drive-in window without even getting out—or on the run. Even if it is brought home to eat, there will never be any dirty dishes to wash because of the handy disposable wrappings. Children, especially, love fast food because it's finger food, no grappling with knives and forks, no annoying instructions from adults about table manners.

As for traveling Americans, a traditionally mobile people in a very large country, the familiar golden arches, Mexican "taco" hats, and "leaning towers" of pizza are reassuring signs that make them feel at home away from home. Even boring, repetitious food is okay, Americans seem to have decided, as long as it is recognizable and dependable. No wonder Ray Kroc unashamedly titled his McDonald's success-story autobiography *Grinding It Out*.

FAST FOOD NUTRITION

What about the nutrition in a standard fast food meal of a burger, fries, and a Coke or shake? Fast feeders argue that the meat patty, lettuce and tomato, enriched bun, and potatoes are honest foods offering protein, carbohydrates, vitamins, and minerals. But let's take a closer look. The beef patty is shockingly expensive protein on a cost per ounce basis, the lettuce and tomato are minimal, a token gesture toward supplying a ration of salad for the guilt-ridden, the bun is basically bleached white flour and air, and the fries are overloaded with grease and salt. They are also low in the nutriment that a baked or boiled potato would supply because high-heat frying and long standing tend to destroy their vitamin C and other nutrients. One particular fast food risk is the too-often reheated fat used in deep frying. Smoking or rancid oil commonly causes only indigestion, but recent studies indicate that it may also have carcinogenic effects.

No one seems able to defend the cola drink with its sugar (or saccharin) and caffeine. And the fast food shake, which is carefully *not* called a milkshake, contains mainly water, saturated fat, emulsifiers, thickeners, sugar, and artificial flavoring. Nor do the brine-soaked pickle slices or "special" sauces thickened with gum tragacanth add any nutritive pluses. In short, the typical fast food meal is high in sugar, salt, saturated fat, and additives. Although it may offer some protein, it is generally low in calcium, iron, fiber, and vitamins A, C, D, and E.

At the same time, it contributes about 1,000 calories to our daily intake, more than one-third of the average requirement for males eleven years and up, and nearly half of the daily requirement for females aged eleven and up. An occasional binge at the burger stand isn't going to ruin one's health, but it's pretty clear that a too-steady fast food diet is poorly balanced and carries a lot of empty calories—far too many for the food value it provides.

Of course, all fast food isn't hamburgers. But it's questionable whether the typical fried chicken, fried fish, hot dog, chili, or taco meal can be any better balanced nutritionally, for most lack whole grains, fresh fruits and vegetables, and milk.

In addition, the flavors of the food specialties presented tend to have been processed out by design. In order to appeal to the widest possible range of eaters, the industry has had to find an acceptable common denominator. So fish, which has had a bad name with many Americans because of its "fishy" taste, has been rendered almost flavorless by the seafood chains and is served up in slabs that taste more of breading and fat than of fish. And Mexican food, which the chains considered too "hot" for the average American taste, has lost its character and been "de-spiced" into an unauthentic blandness.

EATING THE SCENERY

What their food may lack in the way of flavor and character, many of the new sit-down eateries try to make up for in the decor. The "theme restaurant" is one of the latest developments in the fast food industry. A fish-and-chips outlet may be done up as a sea pirate's lair, or a family-style steak house may be a replica of an Old West gambling parlor. English pubs, Mexican haciendas, and even Victorian railroad stations are among today's most popular "dinner house" themes. Usually molded plastic masquerades as rough oak beams, yet the scenery tries hard to make the food taste more authentic than it is. Nevertheless, the chain-run dinner houses serve the same kind of assembly-line meals that the fast food takeouts do. Food arrives in the restaurant kitchen prepackaged, in individual portions, and often precooked, requiring just a quick browning or a few seconds heating in a microwave oven. No chef presides over the kitchen, merely a staff of attendants who work from printed timing instructions.

Even some of the more elite restaurants, with fancy menus, formal waiters, and high prices are not above serving prefrozen beef burgundy and lobster à la Newburg supplied by the same corporate kitchens that prepare airline meals.

How can you tell, short of visiting the kitchen, if you're getting mass-produced glop at gourmet prices? Small, family-run restaurants more often prepare honest food from scratch. And critical taste buds, not dulled by a regular diet of unimaginative, standardized food, can usually spot the difference between the thinly disguised TV dinner and a well-cooked meal prepared with quality ingredients.

To help restaurant patrons know what they're paying for, several American cities have recently proposed "truth-in-menu" bills. Restaurants would have to indicate on their menus any dish that wasn't made in their own kitchens, and would also have to reveal the additives they used, such as MSG, in preparing various dishes. Such proposals may not pass easily into law, but through alerting the public to deceptive practices they may help to stem the advance of high-priced fast food served on white tablecloths.

THE FAST FOOD SCHOOL LUNCH

Having successfully sneaked past the head waiters and white-hatted chefs of so-called haute cuisine restaurants, it isn't surprising that fast food has boldly charged into school cafeterias. Of course, the soggy steam-table vegetables, ragged meat in lumpy gravy, tough Jell-O, and gluey rice pudding formerly served in so many school lunchrooms must have helped to pave the way for the McDonald's-type menus that schools have begun to offer.

In New York City, the Board of Education actually announced in 1977 that several high school kitchens would convert from conventional, old-fashioned hot lunches to burgers, pizzas, tacos, french fries, and shakes. School authorities argued that giving the students something they liked would eliminate waste and keep them in the school cafeteria at lunchtime rather than out at the local burger or hot dog stand. And they promised to serve "nutritionally enriched" fast food—vitamin supplements in the french fries and even some powdered milk in the shakes. One important consideration was to increase cafeteria revenues, both from those students who paid for their lunches and those whose lunches were subsidized through federal and local funding.

But in many parts of the country there have been growing complaints from parents, teachers, and nutritionists about the food served to children at school breakfasts and lunches—sugar-coated cereals, doughnuts, white bread, fried foods, cured meats containing nitrites, and canned fruit in heavy syrup. In addition, vending machines in the school corridors sell candy, gum, ice cream, and soda pop. What's the point, educators say, of teaching nutrition in the classroom if the student then heads directly for the school cafeteria or vending machine that panders to the tastes developed by the junk food and fast food industries?

With so many families opting out of eating meals at home, the school appears to be the only place left that can take an effective stand toward teaching better eating, in both theory *and* practice. The battle may be a tough one, in which the earnest consumer advocate, concerned with the health of future generations, is pitted against the rich and influential food corporation, concerned with the next profit statement. But already parent groups and school officials around the country have begun banding together to introduce nourishing soups and salads, whole-grain breads, fresh fruits, carrot cake or oatmeal cookies instead of Twinkies, fruit juice or fruited milk nogs instead of Hawaiian Punch, into school cafeteria menus.

"Grab 'em while they're young" has been the approach used by the big food corporations for generations; now health food followers, too, have decided it's time to get into the act.

5 HEALTH FOOD FACTS AND FANCIES

What do we mean by "health food" and can we assume that anything we buy in the health food store is better for us than what we buy in the supermarket? Does being a health food fan mean living on dried seaweed and brewers' yeast, raw honey, and fertile eggs? Does it mean following a special diet? Does it mean loading up on vitamins and all those other pills, capsules, and extracts that line the shelves of health food stores? And does any of it look appetizing or taste good?

Health food is one of those stretchable terms that can be made to fit a wide variety of eating styles, some of which are faddist and some of which are grounded in solid scientific fact. Back in the 1920s people believed earnestly in the health benefits of foods like spinach and milk. Spinach was rich in calcium and iron, and milk was the "perfect" food. But what we have learned since is that the naturally occurring oxalates (chemical compounds) in spinach bind up the calcium and make much of it unavailable to the body. Spinach also contains some natural nitrates and nitrites, the very substances that we have denounced as cured-meat preservatives.

This doesn't mean that spinach is poisonous, for calcium can be derived from other foods, and its nitrites are considered less carcinogenic than those in meats. Spinach is still a worthwhile part of a balanced diet, but its exceptional health claims of an earlier day *were* rather exaggerated.

Cow's milk, we now know, is not a perfect food—except for calves. It not only lacks enough vitamin C and iron to maintain optimum health all by itself, but it is often allergenic to human infants. Also, it cannot be properly digested by many people once they are beyond the infant years. Adults of various racial groups, including most Africans and Asians, do not produce enough of the digestive enzyme, lactase, which breaks down the complex sugar in milk, called lactose. Lactose-intolerant individuals may actually become ill with intestinal cramps, bloating, and diarrhea after drinking a glass of milk.

Other fallacies of the 1920s and 1930s included the idea that sugar was actually nourishing because the body absorbed it so readily that it supplied almost instant calories, which were interpreted as "quick energy." Will some of the foods we think of as unimpeachably healthful nowadays begin to get bad notices in the years ahead? Very likely. Let's take a look at some of the widely touted "health" foods of recent times and see how they stand up to the latest scientific findings.

HONEY AND RAW SUGAR

Honey is a prominent item on the shelves of today's health food stores, based on the popular belief that because it is closer to nature than refined white sugar it contains substantial vitamins and minerals that have been processed out of sugar. But honey, whether it is clover, alfalfa, buckwheat, or one of the more delectable-sounding flavors, has only very small traces of B vitamins, calcium, and iron. It is composed mainly of invert sugar, sucrose, maltose, and fructose, and the chemical breakdown inside our bodies renders it hardly any different than "empty calorie" crystal-line white sugar. Honey is also even sweeter than cane or beet sugar.

Some health food fans believe that raw honey, which unlike most supermarket honey is processed from the comb under very moderate rather than high heat, contains impor-tant enzymes. But even if raw honey is rich in this respect (depending on its origin), its enzymes are destroyed when it is used in baking or even heated to 140 degrees Fahrenheit. So unless we plan to eat quantities of raw honey from the jar, we might just as well buy one of the cheaper supermar-ket brands.

The overall fallacy in considering honey a health food, despite its delicious flavor and convenient pouring consis-tency for pancakes, waffles, and desserts, is that it is a highly concentrated sugar, and that it produces dental cavities and carries all the other health risks of refined sugar.

Raw sugar, another supposedly healthful sweetener, isn't really as close to nature as some of us would like to think, for the FDA bans the sale of truly raw cane products due to the molds, insects, and fibers that cling to them. What passes for raw sugar on the store shelf is a pale-tan, refined sugar with a high price tag but a nutritive value close to that of white sugar, for government regulations require that it consist of at least 96 percent sucrose. Also very high in sucrose content is brown sugar, which is simply white sugar that has had a little molasses added to it for coloring and flavoring.

The real nutrients of the sugarcane plant are found in molasses, the dark-brown runoff of the refining process. Blackstrap molasses, the darkest grade, is richest in B vita-mins, calcium, phosphorus, and iron, and was highly recommended by health food advocates back in the 1930s and 1940s. But molasses still contains substantial sucrose, there are better sources of its nutrients, and its flavor is quite strong and slightly bitter. Many of today's health food followers are not enthusiastic about molasses because of the intensive extracting process by which it is produced.

Maple syrup, a closer-to-nature sweetener, has been found suspect by nutritionists due to such processing hazards as paraformaldehyde pellets (placed in tree tapholes to keep the sap flowing) and lead-soldered joints in the metal evaporating pans (and often in the cans in which the syrup is sold). Residues of both harmful paraformaldehyde and poisonous lead can leach into the maple syrup.

Like honey, maple syrup is mainly sugar and has only small traces of nutrients. Its flavor is especially rich and pleasing but it is very high priced because of the short sap-flowing season and the large amount of sap that has to be boiled down to produce the syrup. And, unfortunately, the boiling process itself destroys much of the food value of the sap.

The maple-flavored pancake syrups sold in supermarkets are much cheaper, of course, than pure maple syrup. Like other pancake syrups they are mainly sucrose syrup or corn syrup. A touch of either real maple syrup or artificial maple flavoring is added, and on reading the label we usually learn that additives such as coloring and preservatives are also present.

The problem with all of these sweeteners, even though derived from natural sources and regardless of whether they are very lightly or very heavily processed, is that they are high in sugar content and offer poor nutrition at best. None can really be recommended as health foods to be eaten in unlimited quantities. A much better choice of "something sweet" would be fresh fruit, which is also rich in vitamins, minerals, water, and fiber, and can truly be considered health food.

If fresh fruits are good for us, are dried fruits even better? While dried figs, dates, apricots, prunes, and other moist, chewy morsels certainly contain more nourishment than additive-laden candy, fruits do lose nutritive value in the drying process. Also, because dried fruits are 65 to 75 percent sugar and tend to stick to the teeth, they are as guilty as caramels and taffies when it comes to causing cavities.

Coloring agents, preservatives, and chemical sprays are often used on dried fruits. Sulfur dioxide acts as a bleaching agent to keep apples, pears, apricots, and golden raisins light colored; sorbic acid is employed as a preservative; and imported dried fruits are fumigated to prevent the transmission of insects and plant diseases. Dates are usually pasteurized to prevent mold.

Unbleached, preservative-free dried fruits command higher prices, and are usually found in health food stores. They should be kept in the refrigerator rather than on the pantry shelf. Although not for calorie-watchers and not really health foods, dried fruits do have an advantage over candy and gum as naturally good-tasting and satisfying snacks.

RAW MILK AND FERTILE EGGS

When it comes to dairy products and eggs, many health food followers hold out staunchly for the "natural" product. They claim that pasteurization, because of the high temperature used, destroys the vitamin C and the natural enzymes in milk. However milk is a poor source of vitamin C to begin with, and no one is quite sure of the value of the enzymes in cow's milk. They may be of benefit only to the calf, or of no benefit at all. Pasteurization does effectively kill the organisms that cause tuberculosis, typhoid fever, diphtheria, and other serious diseases, and almost all milk sold in the United States is pasteurized.

The exception is government-certified raw milk, unpasteurized milk that comes from frequently inspected cows and is produced under highly sanitary conditions. But, as fewer and fewer states have wanted to bother with the inspection routines, certified milk is getting harder to find. Some health food fans have turned to buying unpasteurized milk directly from a farmer whom they trust, but raw milk from an uninspected source carries risks regarding freshness and wholesomeness, and could turn out to be quite unhealthy after all.

Another dairy product high on the health food list is yogurt. All commercial varieties are, of course, made with pasteurized milk to which a bacterial culture is added for a custardlike consistency and a slightly acid tang. Early in the century the Russian biologist, Élie Metchnikoff, noticed that Bulgarian peasants, who ate a great deal of yogurt, were very long-lived. We realize today, though, that there were other factors of diet, life-style, and heredity that kept hundred-year-old Bulgarians active and healthy, and that most of the claims made for yogurt have been exaggerated.

One advantage is that yogurt, which is similar in food value to milk, is easier for lactose-intolerant individuals to digest because its milk sugar, lactose, is converted to lactic acid when the souring bacterial culture is introduced. Plain yogurt mixed with fresh fruit or topped with homemade granola makes a nourishing and tasty snack or dessert. But the much more widely eaten flavored yogurts combined with preserves or other sweeteners are more expensive, less nutritious, and considerably higher in calories. Some are as fattening as a slice of layer cake, and can't be considered a health food or a diet food.

A product called Tiger's Milk is a popular health food store item that has nothing to do with tigers and not a great deal to do with milk. The ingredients in the powdered mixture usually include dried skim milk, soybean concentrate to boost protein, brewers' yeast as a source of B vitamins, and other nutrients in concentrated form. Some varieties contain sugar, flavoring, and vegetable gums. Tiger's Milk can be combined with water and whipped into a milkshake-like drink, or it can be added to various recipes. Though its healthful properties are presumably intended to give one the vigor of a tiger, people who eat a well-balanced diet of natural foods will probably find that they are getting plenty of essential nourishment and don't require high-priced supplements or concentrates.

Many of the health food fans who seek out raw milk favor fertile eggs as well—eggs from free-ranging barnyard hens that have been fertilized by the rooster. But the claim that the rooster hormones in fertile eggs make them more nutritious for humans has not been proven. It's quite likely that the male hormones are of value only to the chicks that would otherwise not hatch from the eggs.

Another argument for fertile eggs is that hens raised in an old-fashioned barnyard rather than a modern hatchery receive a more natural and therefore a better diet. But this depends on the barnyard's offering of insects, worms, and other pecking fare, plus the feed the individual farmer supplies. As well-fed hens will lay more eggs than poorly fed ones (whether a rooster is present or not), commercially raised laying hens usually receive a fairly nourishing diet of poultry feed.

At the same time, however, hens living in close-quartered hatcheries also receive antibiotics and tranquilizers to prevent disease and reduce stress, and residues of these substances may appear in the eggs. So the "fertile and organic" egg sold in health food stores, although more expensive than supermarket eggs, may be worth the extra price *provided* we can be sure that the claims made for them are true.

COLD-PRESSED OILS AND STONE-GROUND FLOUR

Before the era of technology, oil was crushed from seeds by pounding them in a mortar, and grain was ground into coarse flour between two stones. Neither of these methods used throughout antiquity was very efficient. Only a limited amount of oil, which rose to the top of the seed mass, was extracted, and the crushed grain was full of coarse husks so that it baked into a dark, dense loaf. But the oil was pure and natural, and the flour retained all the nutrients and fiber of the whole grain. The oil was known as "cold-pressed," as it was extracted without the use of heat, and the flour was "stone-ground."

In the nineteenth century, with the advent of high-powered machinery, it became possible to press, grind, purify, and refine raw foodstuffs as never before. Oil is today extracted from seeds by intense pressure, or with the aid of chemical solvents. In modern oil production, the seeds are often heated beforehand to soften them, and the pressing itself generates high temperatures. Solvent-extracted oil must be boiled to drive off the chemical, which is usually petroleum-based.

Yet today it is possible once again to buy oils that are labeled "cold-pressed," and many health food fans favor them because it has been discovered that the high heat used in processing oil tends to destroy both its vitamin E content and its lecithin. Lecithin, a natural substance found in plant and animal tissues, acts as an antioxidant, preventing the oil from turning rancid.

Since it is very unlikely that any oil sold nowadays has been truly cold-pressed—by manual or simple mechanical pressure as in the distant past—what the label probably means is that the oil has been produced at 150 degrees Fahrenheit rather than 450 degrees. So some vitamin E will have been lost, although not as much as in those popular supermarket brands that are extremely pale in color, odorless, have a long shelf life, don't need to be refrigerated, and are recommended for high-heat deep-fat frying. The more highly refined the oil, the less nutritious it is likely to be. And because the natural preservatives in the oil—the vitamin E and lecithin—have been largely processed out, synthetic antioxidants like BHT and BHA are sometimes added to highly refined oils.

Less-refined oils are likely to be richer in vitamin E and lecithin, even though they have not been *truly* cold-pressed. These more nutritious oils are usually deeper in color and should have a faint odor of the corn, olives, peanuts, sesame seeds, or other natural oil sources from which they were extracted.

Whole-grain, stone-ground flour is possibly as much of a myth in twentieth-century America as cold-pressed oil, but for a different reason. In old-fashioned stone grinding of flour, by water, wind, or other naturally powered method, so many coarse particles of bran husk and wheat germ are left in the flour that the miller usually has to sieve out a substantial portion. This means that the flour doesn't contain *all* of the wheat berry and isn't truly "whole grain."

On the other hand, when wheat grain is ground in high-speed roller mills, the whole wheat flour that results does contain all of the original grain in finely pulverized and usable particles. One of the reasons that health food fans champion slow-method stone grinding is that they believe the heat generated by high-speed milling destroys some of the nutrients in the grain. But as no studies have yet proven this point, paying a higher price for a package of flour labeled "stone-ground" may be a fallacy

The health food fan's preference for whole wheat flour is, however, nutritionally justified. White flour is milled from the endosperm, the portion of the wheat berry in which food is stored for the growth of the seed. The endosperm contains mostly starch and a little protein, while the discarded bran and germ have most of the minerals and vitamins, and the germ also contains protein as well as an oil rich in vitamin E.

To make matters even worse, most white flour is bleached after milling to make it snowy white instead of its natural creamy color. The purely cosmetic bleaching is done with chemicals that are presumably harmless, but that do destroy what little vitamin E there is in the endosperm.

Even the enrichment of white flour with three synthetic B vitamins (thiamin, riboflavin, and niacin) plus iron does not restore to it the food value of whole wheat flour. For some 22 nutrients, including vitamin E, calcium, phosphorus, and trace minerals, have been removed with the bran and germ, and only four have been put back. With the public's growing realization that today's puffy white loaves, buns, and cakes are nutritionally impoverished, whole-grain baked goods—once spurned as the coarse and unrefined food of the poor—are coming back into favor as part of the movement toward natural foods.

SEAWEED AND SEA SALT

The public, however, is probably a lot less ready to follow health food enthusiasts who are partial to the vegetable foods of the briny deep. Eating seaweed comes out of the Japanese tradition, for the people of that crowded island-nation long ago discovered that it was an excellent source of iodine and also rich in calcium, phosphorus, iron, and many trace minerals.

Large-leafed reddish dulse, dark-stranded hiziki, and granulated brown-green kelp are just a few of the popular dried seaweeds. Kelp, which is also available in leaf and tablet form, is added to all sorts of dishes from baked goods to soups and salads. Some health food fans use it as a mild salt substitute, for it is only slightly salty and not as fishy-tasting as the stronger-flavored seaweeds that go into soups, salads, and vegetable dishes.

Provided one likes the taste, seaweed can be a healthful addition to the diet. The only hazard is that an overabundance in the diet might supply too much iodine. Like too little iodine, an excess could cause goiter, a swelling of the thyroid gland in the neck. But the danger is considered minimal.

Much more common is goiter from too little iodine in the diet, which occurs mainly in inland and mountainous regions where the soil in which food is grown contains little or none of this essential mineral. The symptoms of iodine deficiency, in addition to goiter, include lethargy, weight gain, dry skin, and brittle hair. Iodine-deficient mothers may give birth to retarded, deformed children, known as cretins. Goiter has been largely wiped out in the United States by adding potassium iodide to table salt, known as iodized salt.

Most of the commercially sold table salt in the United States comes from inland salt springs or salt mines. Health food followers, however, often favor sea salt, salt that has been evaporated from sea water. Oddly enough, although sea salt contains many minerals that are not present in salt from inland sources, it does not contain much iodine and cannot be counted on to prevent goiter. So most of the sea salt sold today is iodized and some of it even contains chemicals to make it free-flowing.

Unlike seaweed, sea salt cannot really be considered a health food. Whatever natural trace minerals it may contain, it is still salt. As in the case of sweeteners, even if they come from natural sources, it should be used sparingly.

VITAMIN MIRACLES AND MYTHS

With the discovery early in the twentieth century that vitamins were the magical elements behind the cures for scurvy, rickets, beriberi, and other serious deficiency diseases, vitamins came to be regarded not only as essential for good health but as cures for an even wider variety of ailments. Vitamins had, of course, been around since life began and had supported human populations for eons simply through the food they ate. But once scientists identified and isolated these substances, and learned how to synthesize or concentrate them in the laboratory into pills and capsules, "popping" vitamins became enormously popular.

Today health-conscious Americans ingest vast quantities of vitamin tablets on the theory that if a little is good more is better, and for a broad variety of personal reasons. They take a daily multivitamin pill, and give one to their children, to ease a bad conscience about eating junk food or a poorly balanced diet; because they distrust the food supply;

or "just to make sure" that they remain healthy. Or they concentrate on extra-large doses of one particular vitamin—vitamin A to improve eyesight, vitamin C to prevent colds, B vitamins for more pep and energy, vitamin E to increase sexual potency and slow down the aging process.

Not surprisingly, laboratory-produced vitamins have become big business, for the large drug companies play on the fears, guilts, and misunderstandings of the public, and the public responds with, "Oh well, why not? They can't hurt me and they might even help." Even some doctors prescribe vitamin supplements for patients with vague or general complaints, since the mere act of taking a daily dose of something seems to make some patients feel better.

Do vitamin pills really do all those things that are claimed for them? And, if we are eating a well-balanced diet of natural or very lightly processed foods, do we really need vitamins to supplement those that come to us in such wide range and ample quantity directly from our dinner plates?

The answer according to most medical and health authorities is no, most of us should not require vitamin supplements. The only individuals in our society who may regularly need extra vitamins are alcoholics, habitual users of certain drugs, people with digestive-absorption problems and other rare illnesses, some pregnant women and nursing mothers, some infants on feeding formulas other than mother's milk, and people who live on very limited, poorly balanced diets such as white rice, white flour, and sugar, or on a fad diet of a single food such as brown rice.

Even if vitamin pills may not be doing us any good, is there any harm in taking them anyway? Yes, there may be. Fat-soluble vitamins like A, D, E, and K are stored in our bodies. Vitamins A and D in excess can have toxic effects that are medically well documented. An overdose of vitamin A over an extended period can lead to severe headaches and tumorlike pressure in the skull; dry, cracked skin; hair loss; and retarded growth in children. Yet many people take vitamin A supplements because they mistakenly think that since a deficiency causes night blindness an abundance will remedy certain visual problems. Vitamin A, and other vitamins, just don't work that way. Besides we can get all the vitamin A we need from whole milk, cream, butter, cheese, egg yolk, yellow fruits and vegetables, dark-leafed greens, and fish-liver oils. Also, margarines are fortified with vitamin A.

Vitamin D aids the absorption of calcium from the digestive tract and makes it available for building bone and tooth tissue. But too much can retard mental and physical growth in children, cause nausea, hypertension, and hypercalcemia, in which excess calcium is leached from the bones and carried by the bloodstream to the kidneys where it is deposited as kidney stones. In Great Britain, following World War II, a great many infants were malformed and retarded because they received milk and other baby foods that were overfortified with vitamin D under a government program designed to improve the nation's health after years of war shortages.

Sunlight is the main source of vitamin D, and we don't need to be sun worshippers to get enough. It filters into our bodies in a number of ways, both directly and indirectly through the food we eat. In addition, pasteurized milk sold in the United States is commonly fortified with vitamin D, by irradiation through exposure to ultraviolet light.

What about vitamin E, the glamour vitamin supplement of the late twentieth century? Because male laboratory rats deprived of vitamin E have been found to become sterile, it has been dubbed the antisterility vitamin. But despite claims that vitamin E will promote human fertility, improve sexual prowess, cure arthritis, and prevent wrinkles and heart attacks, there is no proof that any of these is valid. The main advantage of vitamin E to humans seems to be its antioxidant action.

We don't know for sure how much supplementary vitamin E (which is easily come by in everyday foods) is too much. It's also a little early to tell what the toxic effects, if any, of megavitamin doses of vitamin E may be, but it is suspected by some researchers to create imbalances in the body in connection with iron, an essential mineral. Seeds, nuts, legumes, whole grains, wheat germ, leafy greens, and vegetable oils that have not been too highly refined or heated to very high temperatures are excellent natural sources of vitamin E.

The last of the fat-soluble vitamins, vitamin K, is responsible for blood coagulation and, as it is in plentiful supply in almost all human bodies, it hasn't become a big over-the-counter seller—yet. Taking a vitamin K supplement, without careful medical supervision, can be extremely dangerous.

Since the B vitamins and vitamin C are water-soluble rather than fat-soluble, any excess amounts are excreted from the body, mainly in the urine. Therefore, it would appear that we don't need to worry about harmful effects from overdoses taken in the form of laboratory-made supplements. But that isn't quite the case.

The eight B vitamins, which include thiamin (B1), riboflavin (B2), pyridoxine (B6), cobalamin (B12), niacin, folic acid, pantothenic acid, and biotin, perform a truly vast and complex range of functions that promote growth and maintain life. However, too much niacin and folic acid have been medically recorded as dangerous. Folic acid can, for one thing, mask the symptoms of pernicious anemia, a serious disease caused by innate problems of vitamin B12 absorption. In any case, the B vitamins are richly supplied in a wide variety of foods—milk, meat, fish, poultry, eggs, fruits and vegetables, whole grains, peanuts and other legumes, and yeast.

As to vitamin C, the antiscurvy vitamin, no studies have as yet proven that massive doses prevent the common cold. But we do have evidence that the enormous vitamin C intake recommended for this purpose can cause diarrhea, is suspected of causing bladder and kidney stones, and poses dangers to diabetics by making it difficult to detect sugar in the urine. As to natural sources, we are all familiar with the high vitamin C content of citrus fruits, tomatoes, green peppers, cabbage, strawberries, cantaloupe, dark green vegetables, and—yes—potatoes, preferably baked or boiled with the skins on.

Another problem with taking manufactured vitamins in high concentrations is that, as in the case of other food additives, little is known about their interaction with each other, with other nutrients, and with substances in the human body. Nevertheless the argument between advocates and opponents of vitamin-supplement-taking rages on.

A further controversy is that between champions of "natural" vitamins (manufactured vitamins derived from natural sources) and those who say that completely synthetic vitamins are just as good. Both come from the laboratory in tablet, capsule, or other "convenience" form and are available on the shelves of drug, discount, supermarket, or health food stores. Both undergo a great deal of processing and contain additives that serve as binders, emulsifiers, and stabilizers, as well as extenders such as cornstarch, flavorings such as sugar, and colorings such as the allergen, Yellow No. 5, which does not even have to be listed on the label.

Although a great many medical authorities say that there is no difference between the body's utilization of synthetic and so-called natural vitamins, enthusiasts who endorse the latter pay considerably higher prices for vitamin A made from carrots, B vitamins made from dried liver, and vitamin C made from rose hips, acerola cherries, or other concentrated natural sources. And even though many "natural" vitamin pills contain some synthetic vitamins to make up their full potency, their supporters insist that they are superior to all-synthetic vitamins because they are absorbed more slowly by the body, are better utilized, are less likely to cause nutrient imbalances, and contain enzymes and trace minerals that are closer to those in vitamin-rich foods, an argument that makes one wonder what's wrong with whole foods as a direct source of vitamins in the first place.

It's quite true that the vitamin values in junk foods and highly processed foods are reduced through refining, overheating, overcooking, and long storage. But with a little more care in our food choices, we can ingest all the vitamins we need as nature meant us to, and also much more cheaply and safely.

The same foods that are good sources of vitamins provide plenty of minerals, inorganic substances that have numerous structural and regulatory functions in the body and that include calcium, phosphorus, iron, potassium, magnesium, and others, as well as the so-called trace minerals, those that we need in very minute quantities. Laboratory-produced mineral supplements can actually be damaging if self-administered, and we should remember that white flour,

white bread, dry cereals, cornmeal, and white-flour macaroni products are already synthetically enriched with iron,
and that salt is often fortified with iodine in the form of
potassium iodide.

The miracles wrought by vitamins in the treatment of
serious deficiency diseases must not be underestimated, but
we should also recognize that many of the vitamin myths
we live by today are based on scientific half-truths. Is it
possible that twentieth-century Americans are caught in a
twin conspiracy devised by the food-processing industry
and the vitamin-pill purveyors? Are we being programmed
to eat mass-produced nonnutritious food and then to clamor
blindly for vitamin and mineral nourishment out of bottles
and jars from the pharmaceutical laboratory? It certainly
seems that way. Perhaps, before real food vanishes from the
scene, we ought to decide to take a firm stand, showing our
preference for natural, whole foods and rejecting any and
all chemicalized concoctions in our diets.

THE HEALTH FOOD BUSINESS

Back in 1965 there were only about 500 health food stores
in the United States. By 1972 their number had increased
sixfold to 3,000. Today the count is anybody's guess, for
there are also health food sections in supermarkets, in discount and department stores, and in gyms and health clubs.
In addition, health food restaurants have sprung up almost
everywhere.

Do we have to buy our food in health food stores to eat
healthfully? Not necessarily. Although supermarket
shelves are lined, by and large, with highly processed,
preservative-laden products, it is also possible to buy wheat
germ, unprocessed bran, whole wheat flour, brown rice,

molasses, clover honey, herb teas, dried peas and beans, raw nuts and seeds, and many other whole foods at our local market, and almost always at lower prices.

Nor are health food stores sanctuaries of everything that is healthful, natural, and additive-free. Flavored protein-booster drink mixes contain carrageenan, crunchy cookies and other baked goods are highly sweetened, and processed sea salt under a health food brand name contains the same synthetic potassium iodide and chemical anticaking agent that iodized supermarket salt does. But it costs a lot more.

People usually gravitate to health food stores for organic foods—pesticide-free and herbicide-free produce grown in naturally fertilized soil, eggs from free-ranging hens, raw milk products, and organically raised poultry and meats. Here the prices really soar, and the question of whether these products are truly organic is ever present. Few of us can examine the poultry farms and dairies that supply the store, conduct independent laboratory tests to find out if there *are* any chemical residues in the food, or check out the feed of the cattle that were the source of the organic chopped beef in the health store's freezer. Nor are there any federal consumer-protection regulations that specifically cover the production or sale of organic food.

Health enthusiasts also need to guard against faddism, remembering that there are no miracle cures in raw honey or blackstrap molasses, dried seaweed or vitamin overdoses. And all of us have to watch out for the word "natural," which hucksters apply loosely to numerous products hoping to hook the newly health-conscious public. Can there really be a "natural" potato chip that has BHT in it, a "natural" fruit drink that contains artificial color? And what is a "natural light beer" or a "natural menthol cigarette?"

Unfortunately, businesses both big and small are all too ready to play on the public's gullibility. So it's possible that even your friendly local health store owner isn't in business entirely for his or her health.

At the same time, health food stores do offer many natural, healthful, and delicious products that are still not found on supermarket shelves, and they should certainly be explored often, provided we shop in them with as much care and discrimination as in the supermarket. There is certainly no question that the health food movement, as a whole, has been highly beneficial to the American food scene, pointing up the evils of junk food, and reviving an interest in home baking and in cooking honest meals with real food from scratch.

Americans have also begun to learn that health food doesn't have to taste or look unattractive, that it can be appetizing as well as nutritious. And, with the introduction of the "new" vegetarianism, the health food movement has begun to offer Americans appealing alternatives to their traditional but health-threatening high-meat diet.

6 MEAT-EATERS VERSUS VEGETARIANS

Red meat is nowadays one of the most talked about items in the American diet. People are concerned about its high cost, its high saturated-fat content, and the risky chemical residues it may harbor as a result of the powerful antibiotics and growth hormones that beef cattle are fed. At the same time, most of us still haunt the meat display case of our local market hunting for a thick, tender-looking steak to add to the cache in the freezer at home. And when we go out to eat at a restaurant our first choice is often a juicy, charcoal-broiled steak.

How did Americans get so addicted to beef that they now eat an average of 95 pounds of it a year? Add 65 pounds of pork per year (about two-thirds of it in the form of cured meats), and about 8 pounds of veal and lamb combined, and you have a grand total of 168 pounds. At that figure, the United States ranks with New Zealand, Australia, Argentina, and Uruguay as one of the five biggest meat-eating countries in the world. And that 168 pounds doesn't include about 50 pounds of chicken per year and nearly 10 pounds of turkey.

Until the first cattle were introduced into the New World by the Spanish conquerors in the late sixteenth century, no beef animals even existed in America. The Indians of what is today the United States did hunt buffalo, bear, elk, moose, deer, and many smaller animals for food. On the other hand, some tribes lived largely on crops of corn, beans, and squash, and others who were not farmers and who lived in the semiarid, game-scarce Southwest grubbed for roots and gathered berries, nuts, acorns, and the young green shoots of plants. Their "meat" consisted mainly of locusts, honey ants, and other insects.

Even the first European settlers of the eastern seaboard were not big meat-eaters, for meat-eating was reserved for the rich in Europe, and most of the colonists had been poor peasants or town-dwellers in their former homelands. It wasn't until the Texas ranchers of the 1860s began to breed a hybrid beef animal that was part tough, hardy Spanish longhorn and part domesticated English shorthorn that the potential of the excellent feeding grasses of the western rangelands came to be fully realized. During that same period, profitable markets for beef were opening up in the rapidly growing cities of the East, bustling with new immigrants and surging with new industrial wealth. By the 1880s Chicago had become a major meat-slaughtering center, and packers had begun shipping carcasses rather than live animals to Boston and New York in the recently developed railway refrigerator cars.

THE TASTE FOR RED MEAT

Soon Americans were eating steak and mutton chops for breakfast and huge roasts for dinner, while saloons offered the "free lunch," featuring generous helpings of ham, roast beef, and pork sausages, along with pickles, herrings, and other salty foods, to patrons who bought whiskey or beer. Of course, not all Americans could afford such a meat-rich diet, for meat though more plentiful was still far more costly than the bread, potatoes, and watered-down bluish milk of the poor. But meat had become America's symbol of affluence.

In the closing years of the nineteenth century, known as the Gay Nineties, the gentleman with a well-rounded belly spanned by a solid-gold watch chain bespoke prosperity and well-being. His paunchiness was an advertisement for his diet, heavy with the fat of hearty steaks, chops, and roasts, and of pies, puddings, cobblers, and dumplings made with plenty of lard or rendered pork fat.

During the early years of the twentieth century, as people began to learn more about nutrition, it was also discovered that meat contained vitamins, minerals, and high-quality protein, the very substance of every cell in our bodies—bones, blood, skin, muscles, organs, enzymes. Meat wasn't simply a status symbol, a mark of wealth and prestige, any longer; it was considered an essential every-day food for every healthy, red-blooded American.

Keeping up with the national demand for beef, as it began to escalate, was no problem in the first half of the twentieth century. Even though the rangelands had shrunk due to the expansion of farming, while the hungry herds of meat animals had continued to expand, cattlemen found a new way to keep up production. Instead of letting cattle roam the pasturelands until they were heavy enough for slaughter (using up energy as they sought food), the idea of the feedlot was developed.

Soon cattle were being boxed up in feedlot pens for months before slaughter. Standing flank to flank, crowded together with no chance for exercise, they were fed corn, soybeans, and other nourishing grains that added calories the animals could not work off. As America's fertile farm-lands continued to yield grain surpluses year after year, right through to the 1960s, the price of meat didn't go up that much. At the same time, people developed a taste for the much more tender and flavorful meat of grain-fed, feedlot cattle. By comparison, the meat of active cattle fed on wild pasture grasses was dry and stringy, for only a well-fattened animal could produce a nicely marbled steak, one that had plenty of fat distributed throughout the lean of its muscles.

Then, in the early 1970s, a combination of world grain shortages and a growing demand for grain-fed meat among the world's newly affluent people led to an enormous jump in the price of beef and all other meats, as well as grain itself. Prices at the meat counter soared, and they have been rising ever since. From time to time they may dip a little, but the trend is almost sure to continue upward. America's red meat has become the most expensive item in the family food budget.

EATING HIGH ON THE HOG

If we think of livestock animals as machines for converting plant foods into animal products, we can see how really inefficient they are. It takes three to four pounds of grain feed to produce one pound of chicken; it takes about six pounds of grain to produce one pound of pork; and it takes eight to ten pounds of feedlot grain to produce one pound of beef, helping to explain why beef is so much more expensive than chicken or even pork.

We don't think of Americans as being enormous eaters of grain, but actually we are. The average American consumes about 2,000 pounds a year of corn, sorghum, wheat, and other grains—most of it indirectly—in the form of beef, pork, and chicken, while many people on earth, too poor to have a high-meat diet, eat 500 pounds a year of rice, corn, and other common grain staples in *direct* form. They are eating low on the food chain, while we in the meat-eating societies are eating high on the food chain (meat animals feed on plant foods, and we then feed on meat animals).

As the United States is the most highly populated of the big-five meat-eating nations, it consumes about 30 percent of all the meat in the world. Yet it has less than 6 percent of the earth's population. So you could say that, by eating so high on the hog, Americans are hogging the world's food supply in terms of both meat *and* grain. If the United States alone went back to eating pasture-fed cattle—a very unlikely possibility—a tremendous amount of grain could be released for the world's masses of hungry people. And if Americans began to eat even a little less meat than they do now, a great deal of additional land could be turned over to the growing of food for human consumption. As it is, the United States actually imports more than 5 percent of its meat from abroad, mainly to fill the freezer lockers of the booming hamburger chains.

Most of us, though, don't like to think about the moral issues of meat-eating. We tell ourselves that there have always been gaps between the rich and the poor, between the overfed and the starving. Few of us will sit down to a steak dinner or bite into a Big Mac with the thought that a human being is going to bed hungry somewhere in the world because the animal we are eating had to be so generously fed.

We are a lot more likely, however, to be disturbed by the large amount of saturated fat in the steaks, hamburgers, bacon, and hot dogs that we eat. Meat fat may be flavorful and filling, but we repeatedly hear that it is considered responsible for most cases of obesity, for boosted cholesterol levels, and that it is closely linked to heart attacks and cancer, and two principal killer diseases in the United States.

Of course, factors other than animal fats may be responsible for these serious health problems—environmental pollution, smoking, the stress of modern life, excessive sugar or other elements in our diet. But studies show that the Japanese, who get only about 20 percent of their total calories in fat (as opposed to 42 percent in the United States) have far fewer heart attacks, even though they too live in a stressful, industrialized society.

Eating high on the hog the American way does seem to have its penalties, but cutting the fat out of our diets isn't easy. Even a well-trimmed, marbled steak is 15 to 20 percent fat, and we usually have french fries or a buttery, sour cream-topped baked potato with it. Add to this an oily dressing on our salad and a rich dessert, and it's easy to see how the fat calories add up. Other popular meats are even fattier. The government permits up to 30 percent fat in hamburgers and hot dogs, and up to 50 percent fat in pork sausage. Fried chicken is 50 percent fat, contained mainly in the coating, and bacon is at least 75 percent fat.

Studies show that cancer, too, may be related to a high saturated-fat diet. People in all of the top meat-eating countries get much more bowel cancer than do the people of Mexico, Central America, Africa south of the Sahara, and Japan, countries where very little meat but many grains and vegetables are eaten. Yet when Japanese people move to the United States and change their diet from rice, fish, vegetables, and seaweed to meat, their bowel cancer rate begins to rise. Breast cancer may also be related to a diet high in animal fats, particularly those found in dairy products. American women have an eight times higher incidence of breast cancer than do Japanese women.

Even the way Americans cook their meats may be contributing to the high incidence of cancer. Meat fat, when it drips onto hot coals in charcoal broiling, decomposes. Then, as the smoke rises, this chemically altered substance—which is believed to be carcinogenic—is redeposited on the meat. So the crisp, charred surfaces that most of us enjoy so much may actually be dangerous to our health. The deposits of burnt fat on meats broiled in a gas or electric oven, however, do not appear to be cancer-causing.

FEEDLOT FOOD

The fat content of meat isn't the only problem. Whatever drugs, hormones, pesticides, or other chemicals are fed to the cattle, hogs, or poultry that we eat are all too likely to wind up on our dinner plates. Antibiotics, to prevent disease, are a big item in the diets of feedlot cattle, crowded together in pens and kept standing in their own manure. Chickens, too, no longer roam about freely in a barnyard, but are raised in row upon row of small cages, a number of birds confined to a cage. The spread of disease could wipe out hundreds or thousands of food animals, so penicillin and other drugs, many of which are also used in the treatment of human diseases, are generously sprinkled into livestock feed.

Although thorough cooking destroys the potency of most antibiotics, there is a special risk to those of us who eat rare steaks and burgers. Antibiotic residues concentrated in the animal's tissues can cause allergic reactions in humans and can also develop drug-resistant bacteria in the human body, making antibiotics ineffective against serious illnesses.

Tranquilizers used to reduce stress among caged chickens, penned calves, and other mass-produced livestock also turn up in the meat we eat, as do the residues of the pesticides and herbicides with which both grassy rangeland and feed crops are sprayed.

Even more unsettling is the presence of DES (diethylstilbestrol), the female growth hormone, in the meat Americans eat. This substance was first synthesized in Great Britain in the late 1930s and was further developed at Iowa State University. As early as 1947, poultry growers were implanting DES pellets in the necks of chickens. But this practice was banned in 1959 after a male restaurant worker who ate a diet high in chicken necks (which were given to him free) began to develop marked female characteristics of the body. DES was approved for use as an additive to cattle feed in 1954.

The reason cattle, sheep, and poultry growers immediately became enthusiastic about DES was that the hormone made the conversion of livestock feed into meat much more efficient, so that animals became plumper and meatier more quickly on less or cheaper feed. Giving DES to cattle actually caused their weight to increase by 10 percent or more. It wasn't until 1971 that the cancer-causing properties of DES came to public attention. Young women whose mothers had taken DES in drug form on the advice of their doctors in the 1950s, in order to prevent miscarriage, were found to have a rare form of vaginal cancer. The cancer-causing properties of DES had apparently been passed on to the female embryo in the course of the pregnancy, although it had taken 15 to 20 years for the cancer to show up.

A number of western European countries plus Argentina and Australia quickly banned the use of DES in cattle feed. Although the United States also banned it in 1973, following evidence of high residues in beef liver, beef kidneys, and muscle tissue, the ban was overturned on a technicality in 1974.

DES is still in use in the United States today. Cattle growers are, however, supposed to withdraw it from the animal's feed at least seven days before slaughter to keep the residues low. But meats can only be spot-checked for DES, and no one is certain as to what a "safe" level of this potent hormone may be, provided any level is safe. We do know that beef liver, in which the highest concentrations are found, can have about ten times the amount of DES residue that is found in muscle tissue.

Even if DES were to be banned, there are numerous other synthetic compounds of a similar nature waiting in the wings, And United States cattle growers warn that without a growth-booster of some sort beef would cost the consumer even more than it does today because of the increasingly high cost of livestock feed.

Meantime, meat-eaters can only wait and wonder about the effect of DES in their food supply, for cancers—unlike the various types of food poisoning—do not show up overnight. They can take a decade or more to develop. With this and other health risks in mind regarding meat-eating in twentieth-century America, the pleasures of the thick, juicy steak, charred black on the outside, pink and tender on the inside, begin to dim just a little.

THE VEGETARIAN CHOICE

The saturated-fat content and concentrations of chemicals in meats have, in fact, been enough to turn some Americans into vegetarians. Others have chosen vegetarianism for moral or religious reasons. They object to the killing of animals and to eating dead flesh, or they belong to religious groups, such as the Seventh Day Adventists, that either forbid or discourage meat-eating.

Vegetarians can be divided into three main groups: strict vegetarians (also called vegans), who do not eat any food of animal origin; lacto-vegetarians, who include milk, cheese, and other dairy products in their diets; and ovo-lacto-vegetarians, who eat eggs as well as dairy products. But none eat meat, poultry, or fish. There are also some highly specialized groups whose diets are restricted to fruits only (strict fruitarians) or grains only (granivores). Such diets tend to be faddist and poorly balanced. But a wide-ranging plant-food diet can be highly nourishing and healthful.

The first question that pops to mind, especially in the case of strict vegetarians, is "what about protein?" We know that protein is essential to build and maintain the body's tissues, and we know that there is protein in plant foods. Yet we've heard that plant proteins are of an inferior quality to animal proteins. So how do strict vegetarians survive?

To understand how proteins work, we need to know that they are made up of chemical substances called amino acids. The human body requires about twenty-two different kinds of amino acids, most of which it can manufacture out of any sort of protein, plant or animal. But there are eight *essential* amino acids that must come as a group, directly from our food, and these are supplied in a complete, properly balanced set of eight by most animal products, which is why we say that meat, fish, eggs, milk, and cheese are "complete" proteins.

Interestingly, strict vegetarians can get around the problem of not eating animal proteins very neatly. Suppose a vegetarian decides to have a peanut butter sandwich for lunch. Peanuts are low in an essential amino acid called methionine and they are not very high in another amino acid called lysine (which is why this plant food would be called an "incomplete" protein). But if the peanut butter is spread on bread made from whole wheat flour, which is high in methionine, and soy flour which is high in lysine, the peanut butter sandwich can provide a complete protein, equivalent to that of meat or eggs. Or the strict vegetarian can use regular whole wheat bread for the peanut butter sandwich and drink a glass of soy milk with the sandwich. Incomplete proteins that work together to form complete sets of amino acids are called complementary proteins. As long as they are eaten in the same meal—not hours apart—our bodies can't tell the difference.

Fortunately nature has provided dozens of these handy combinations that have worked for people on vegetarian diets since human life began—when game was unavailable, before the domestication of animals, and throughout periods of privation. The people of Mexico, who lived for generation after generation on corn (made into tortillas) and beans, never knew that they were using complementary proteins (corn, which is low in the essential amino acid, lysine, plus beans which are high in lysine). But their food combination worked, and although they had few domesticated food animals and very little game, they were well nourished.

Today, because meat is costly and very unevenly distributed between the rich and the poor, most of the world's people are vegetarians all or most of the time. Many who are vegetarians by necessity instead of choice do not get enough protein because they have very little variety in their diets. They must subsist on a single staple of rice or corn or a starchy root vegetable, and sometimes they do not even have enough of that. But given the possibility of combining grains and legumes—such as corn with beans, rice with lentils or dried peas, or wheat with soy products—or combining various legumes with seeds, it is possible to have a protein-rich diet without adding a morsel of meat.

So the complementary plant proteins of the so-called new vegetarians in the United States and other affluent societies aren't really a new invention. It's just that modern nutritional findings now tell us *why* teaming up certain foods provides more and better protein than if any one of these foods were eaten independently.

Lacto-vegetarians get even more of nature's complementary protein bonuses than do strict vegetarians. When lacto-vegetarians combine milk, yogurt, or cheese with whole grain flour, brown rice, potatoes, or legumes like beans or peanuts, the protein value of the two eaten together becomes even greater than the sum of their parts. And, of course, ovo-lacto-vegetarians, who consume eggs as well, receive an additional source of complete protein.

Even strict vegetarians, however, get more than enough protein each day if they eat a well-balanced complementary protein diet. The Recommended Daily Allowance (RDA) of the Food and Nutrition Board, National Academy of Sciences-National Research Council is 45 to 56 grams of protein for males and females aged eleven and up, and these figures provide a generous safety margin above minimum requirements.

The average American, on the other hand, gets "too much" protein—90 to 100 grams per day. Eating extra protein each day is wasteful, for this nutrient cannot be stored in the body as future tissue-building material. The meat-eater's excess 50 grams or so of protein is either burned up as energy, stored as fat, or excreted in the urine.

In the strict vegetarian diet the only nutritional element that appears to be lacking is vitamin B12, which is found mainly in foods of animal origin. But some authorities say that vegetable sources such as fermented soybean products and seaweed do provide some vitamin B12. Other nutritional experts feel that vegans should take a vitamin B12 supplement. Either way, there is the possibility that vegetarians utilize what they do get of this vitamin more efficiently than do meat-eaters.

Because strict vegetarians eat no milk, cheese, or yogurt, soybean "cheese," or tofu, usually plays a big role in their diets. The soybean is even higher in protein value than other legumes, but does not rank as a complete protein because it is slightly deficient in methionine. Yet it is easy to bring soybean products up to complete protein value by combining them with whole grains such as brown rice, which is high in methionine.

Soybean cheese, or curd, is made from soy "milk," soybeans cooked in water, and is formed into large, pale, almost flavorless blocks, sometimes quite firm and sometimes shivery and custardlike, as are the Chinese and Japanese varieties. Vegetarians use tofu in soups, salads, and cooked dishes to which it adds bulk and nutritive value. Tofu is a good source of calcium, another factor that makes it a useful substitute for milk products.

Miso, also of Oriental origin, is another soy product that some vegetarians favor. Made from fermented soybeans plus wheat, barley or other grains, and salt, miso is a black, strongly flavored paste. Spread on whole wheat bread heaped with sprouts and salad greens, it makes a tasty and nutritious sandwich. And a vegetable broth or soup flavored with enzyme-rich miso (stirred in just before serving) is said to calm the taste buds and lighten the stomach.

Tamari, or soy sauce, which also comes from the Far East, originated as the liquid run-off of miso. Many vegetarians and other health fans use tamari for seasoning all sorts of dishes since it, too, contains a little soy protein. Naturally aged tamari made from soybeans, wheat, and salt is preferred over the supermarket brands that contain preservatives.

HIGH FIBER AND BROWN RICE

Diets that are not necessarily vegetarian but that accent certain plant foods have come along as part of the health food revolution. Among them has been the high-fiber diet which became one of the most talked-about regimens of the 1970s.

A couple of generations ago fiber was known as roughage, and it was recommended that bran, whole grains, and fresh fruits and vegetables be included in the diet every day as a cure for constipation and to maintain general good health. However, as the food of twentieth-century America grew steadily more refined and more highly processed, people paid less attention to this suggestion regarding roughage.

Then, in 1970, a British physician, Dr. Denis Burkitt, reported that rural Africans, who ate a high-fiber diet, were free from cancer of the colon (bowel cancer), appendicitis, hemorrhoids, and other problems related to the lower intestinal tract that were plaguing the members of more affluent societies. It seemed that Grandma had been right about roughage after all.

What is fiber and how can it help? Fiber is simply the indigestible portion of certain plant foods—the hemicellulose found in bran, the pectin in apples, and certain other mucilages, gums, and forms of cellulose found in plants. These substances work in the body by absorbing water and thus helping to form softer, bulkier wastes that pass through the large intestine more rapidly and with greater ease.

Some medical authorities believe that infections and inflammations of the colon, as well as cancer, can be prevented by a high fiber intake, and that even cholesterol levels can be lowered by dietary fiber, thus helping to prevent heart attacks. It is also believed that eating more fiber can aid weight reduction, because the food has to be chewed longer and contributes to a sense of fullness in the stomach.

Many of the far-reaching health claims for the high-fiber diet have not been proven. But, always ready to jump on the bandwagon, the food industry soon began adding fiber to a number of processed foods. The most startling example was that of a bread called Fresh Horizons Special Formula, produced by the Continental Baking Company, a subsidiary of ITT. Fresh Horizons contained 7½ percent powdered cellulose made from wood pulp, which is not a natural dietary fiber for human beings and may even prove to be harmful if consumed over an extended period. Even the fibers naturally found in the foods we eat can cause discomfort and bloating if large amounts are introduced into the diet all at once. And an excess of dry fiber, such as bran, may actually clog the digestive tract.

Meat fiber, which *is* digestible, is not considered part of the high-fiber diet. Roughage from natural food sources does have its place as part of a well-balanced diet in which meat may or may not be included. But simply adding fiber to a saturated-fat, sugar-rich, or high-salt diet is unlikely to prevent most of the ills—cancer, heart disease, diabetes, hypertension—that appear to be directly linked to American eating habits.

Especially good sources of fiber, as well as other food values, are unprocessed wheat bran, wheat germ, whole grain breads and cereals, leafy raw vegetables, carrots, broccoli, apples, dried peas and beans, and nuts and seeds.

A diet that tends to be particularly high in fiber content is the raw-food diet that some vegetarians and other health fans follow. The reasoning behind eating raw foods exclusively is that cooking destroys some of the nutritional value of foods. However, short-period pressure cooking of vegetables, steaming over simmering water, or stir-frying in oil cause relatively little nutrient loss and make for easier chewing and digesting, as well as a greater variety of flavors and textures.

Sprouts are a particular favorite of raw-food enthusiasts because wheat berries, alfalfa seeds, mung beans, and other hard-husked, starchy seeds and beans would not otherwise be edible unless they were cooked. A little moisture and a few days' time are all it takes to "raise" crisp, succulent sprouts to put in salads or sandwiches, or just to eat out of hand.

Meat is not recommended on the raw-food diet, although some followers include raw fish, which is a favorite in Japan. The problem with raw meats and poultry is that they may be infected with parasites or bacteria that can cause serious illnesses in humans. Trichinosis is not uncommon in raw pork. Once the trichinella parasite enters the body it can produce nausea, skin rashes, diarrhea, fever, double vision, and even death. Symptoms usually appear about ten days after eating the infected meat. So all fresh pork should be thoroughly cooked, well beyond the pink stage.

Raw beef may contain the bacteria of brucellosis, or undulant fever (also a danger in unpasteurized milk). The symptoms of this disease, which appear within ten to fifteen days, include chills, fever, aches, and sweats. Eating raw chopped beef is especially risky if the meat has been ground on the same machine as pork, for this adds the possibility of trichinosis infection.

About half the chickens sold in the United States today are infected with salmonella bacteria. However, they pass federal inspection because cooking kills the bacteria, and it is assumed that chicken will not be eaten raw. Careless handling of raw chicken, though, can transmit salmonellosis to humans via other foods. Raw, cracked eggs may also carry the bacteria. Symptoms of salmonellosis, which usually come on within twenty-four hours and are often confused with "24-hour virus" stomach upsets, are nausea, vomiting, fever, abdominal cramps, and diarrhea.

A great deal of bad publicity has been directed in recent years at the macrobiotic diet, sometimes called "Zen macrobiotic," although it is not related to the Eastern religion of Zen Buddhism. Introduced by Japanese-born George Ohsawa, who died in 1966 at the age of seventy-three, the diet divides foods into categories known as yin and yang.

Macrobiotic followers attempt to balance yin and yang foods in their diets, and by slowly simplifying their choices they are supposed to progress through a series of numbered diets to the "highest," or number +7, consisting of brown rice and a little green tea. Unfortunately, many counterculture young people of the 1960s, seeking the promised spiritual enlightenment that was supposed to accompany the nutritionally deficient "brown-rice" diet, developed serious health problems. Some actually died of malnutrition.

Today, under a looser interpretation, many followers claim that macrobiotic eating is not unlike a good natural-foods diet that rejects all processed foods and refined sugar, and emphasizes vegetables, whole grains, nuts, and legumes. Animal foods may be included from time to time but are eaten in smaller amounts than plant foods.

From meat-eaters to vegetarians to food faddists on fringe diets, Americans seem to be searching for fulfillment, health, even salvation through food. And, surely, in a country with as rich and varied a food supply as ours, it does seem (for those of us who can afford it) that we have a completely free choice of what we eat.

But do we really? No examination of how Americans eat today would be complete without a look at the giant food industry, and the ways in which we are all manipulated by it from the moment we take our first sip of baby formula or are propped up to view our first television program.

THE BIG BUSINESS OF FOOD

Ten thousand different items line the shelves, fill the bins, and are displayed in the freezer, meat, and dairy cases of our favorite supermarkets. So it's rather hard to believe that Americans are in any way limited as to what they can buy once they've walked through the magic-eye doors into the temperature-controlled, fluorescent-lit, piped-music atmosphere of one of these massive stores.

Just take a stroll down the cereal aisle. You'll find as many as 150 different kinds of ready-to-eat cereal and dozens of kinds of cooking cereals. Sodas and soft drinks, canned soups and vegetables, macaroni products, cake mixes, salad dressings, frozen dinners, baby food, catfood, and dogfood also appear in great variety, as do food items in scores of other categories. If that isn't choice, what is?

On the other hand, have you ever wondered why it's so difficult to find fresh peas in the pod or fresh rhubarb in season in the produce department, fresh-killed rather than frozen turkeys even at Thanksgiving time, or more than two or three varieties of so-called fresh fish (more often prefrozen and thawed rather than truly fresh)? Why are there thirty or more different brands of beer in the store but only a couple of different kinds of apples—usually Delicious and McIntosh—in a land that as recently as the 1960s grew and marketed more than twenty-five commercial apple varieties, each a unique eating experience?

The answer lies in the powerful control of our food supply by giant companies that decide what will be marketed and what you and I will eat solely on the basis of profitability—theirs. As we've already seen in looking back at the packaging revolution, the advances in food technology, and the resulting onslaught of convenience and junk foods, there is much more money to be made from the sale of highly processed, mass-produced, standardized food than from fresh foods. The latter, unless they are sold quickly, are highly perishable, while frozen and other processed foods have a long storage and shelf life.

Even if a small farm half a mile down the road from a giant supermarket tried to sell its fresh produce, newly laid eggs, or freshly killed chickens to the store's manager, chances are the farmer would be turned down flat, for the big chain stores and the major food wholesalers have special trade arrangements, and interlopers are not welcome. If independent suppliers offer better quality and more variety in fruits, vegetables, poultry, eggs, dairy products, and other items, they are doubly unwelcome.

The trend in the food business is toward bigness and the lessening of competition. Small local or regional food companies that once produced superior baked goods, ice cream, or ethnic foods (Italian, Mexican, Chinese, Jewish) have nearly all been bought up by the corporate conglomerates, large companies consisting of many subdivisions. The brand names have usually remained the same, but often the manufacturing process has been so streamlined that flavor and quality have been sacrificed along the way.

Nevertheless, brand names that sound folksy, ethnic, or personal are favored by the nation's big food companies. Kraftco's Cracker Barrel cheese, Borden's Old London snacks, Hershey's San Georgio Italian foods, Beatrice's La

Choy Chinese foods, Procter & Gamble's Duncan Hines cake mixes, and General Mills' Betty Crocker products are just a few examples.

CORPORATE CONTROL OF FOOD

Once inside the supermarket, we are in the tightly governed realm of the big food corporations. At first glance it may appear that those heavily stocked shelves of breakfast foods and other products are a battleground of the brands. But a closer look will usually reveal that numerous "competing" products are made by the very same company, and that a few giant corporations control the entire market. This is the case of the four huge cereal-makers—Kellogg, General Mills, General Foods, and Quaker Oats. By means of a shared monopoly, the "big four" control 90 percent of the sales in the cereal aisle of the store where you shop.

Even competition *among* the four cereal magnates is minimized, for the group seems to have a long-standing "gentleman's agreement" to amicably divide the spoils of the profitable ready-to-eat cereal business. Supermarkets don't mind alloting a tremendous amount of shelf space to the bulky, brightly labeled boxes of the big four, for they can be sure of a rapid turnover and a good profit. The companies' TV advertising, "free inside" gifts, "boxtop" offerings, and other enticements guarantee an avid buying public that, in the past few decades, has been especially influenced by children's demands for presweetened cereals.

Although the Federal Trade Commission (FTC) has threatened legal action against the cereal monopoly, it seems unlikely that any drastic change will come about, for the cereal companies are not the only big food corporations that are guilty of industrial concentration.

A single company, Campbell, controls 90 percent of the canned soup market. Gerber sells 65 percent of all the baby food in the United States. Three companies produce over half the beer sold in the country (and the outside competition continues to shrink rapidly, from about eighty companies in 1970 to about forty at present). As to soft drinks, five giants—Coca-Cola, Pepsico, Seven-Up, Dr. Pepper, and Royal Crown—have over 75 percent of the market.

Another monopolistic development in the food business is something called "vertical integration," whereby a company that cans pineapple or sells frozen fried chicken takes over the entire cycle of growing, processing, packing, transporting, and sometimes even retailing. By buying up pineapple plantations, shipping lines, can- and label-manufacturing firms, warehouses, and trucking outfits, a pineapple canner is able to assume control of the entire operation from seedling to supermarket. In the case of a fried-chicken integrator, the company may own its own feed-manufacturing factories, chicken hatcheries, chicken farms, and processing plants. At the same time, it may operate its own fried-chicken fast food chain, run a food-service company that supplies hotels, airlines, and institutions, *and* stock the freezer of your neighborhood supermarket.

Corporate control of the food we eat not only robs the consumer of a real variety of choices, reduces quality, and fixes prices through the elimination of meaningful competition, but it also robs the farmer of a competitive market for his products and dictates what the farmer must grow. Few farmers have the opportunity to sell directly to the public, and none can afford to grow what the food packers and processors refuse to buy.

So farmers obediently grow firm, bruise-resistant tomatoes, rot-resistant lettuce, and the kinds of peas, green beans, corn, and other vegetables that are best for canning or freezing, even though they may not be the most tender or flavorful varieties. The turkey farmer who wants to sell his birds to one of the big companies that supply more than 90 percent of the nation's turkeys knows that he had better be raising White Holland turkeys—the only one of the six native American breeds that is commercially desired. In fact, like most poultry farmers nowadays, the turkey breeder is not likely to be an independent farmer in the true sense, but a contracted hireling of a gigantic vertically integrated company.

Vertical integration has also brought about the takeover of family-run farms by agribusinesses, huge corporations like Tenneco, Dow Chemical, and Getty Oil, that not only supply synthetic fertilizers, herbicides, pesticides, plastic wrap and other produce-packaging materials, but operate combined tracts of formerly independent landholdings as vast corporate farms with hired laborers. California has become one of the largest centers of agribusiness operations in the country. But the number of family farms is decreasing everywhere in the United States, from close to 7 million in 1930 to about 2 million at present.

In spite of hard work, efficient management, and modern mechanized equipment, today's independent farmer is being squeezed out by rising production costs, limited markets, the built-in risk of poor weather, losses due to lack of diversification of crops, and a steadily declining share of the consumer dollar.

For every dollar the food shopper spent in 1977, the farmer got an average of 39 cents. The remaining 61 cents was absorbed all along the route from the farm to the retail store by "middleman" costs like fuel, transportation, labor, warehousing, packaging, and even the Muzak and energy-guzzling open-shelf freezer cases in your supermarket. Today, despite rising retail food prices, the farm-to-retail price spread is increasing, and the farmer is getting proportionately less.

When it comes to processed foods, the farmer's share is even smaller. The family of a dairy farmer pays at least five times more for an ice cream cone than it received for the milk that went into it; a wheat farmer pays at least eight times more for a loaf of bread than the amount of money that was received for the wheat.

So every time a consumer buys a package of processed food, most of what he or she spends tumbles into the widening gap between the farmer and the consumer. It is the food-processing industry that reaps the principal benefit. And because of high profitability, food processors are encouraged to pursue an even vaster market by expanding their range of products.

FUTURE FOOD

New products are the lifeblood of the food industry. They are easily financed because research, advertising, packaging, "free introductory" offers, and other costs are easily passed on to the bedazzled consumer who pays for both the quickly buried failures and the successes.

Not content with offering simply-processed foods like canned fruit cocktail and frozen meat patties, the food industry has also given us those hundreds of complex convenience foods with which we are all familiar—dehydrated mixes, synthetic juices, nondairy creamers, and "instant" breakfasts that taste like candy bars.

What will the next phase be? Although most of us don't

realize it, the foods of the future are already with us. Take that pizza you had for lunch. Bread, tomatoes, and cheese are what you thought you ate. But you might have been chewing away on imitation cheese made from coconut oil, cereal solids, caseinates that were chemically derived from milk, various salts, and artificial flavoring and coloring. The tomato sauce may never have been near a real tomato. Chemically blended starches and acids, synthetically flavored and colored, can simulate tomato bases in spaghetti sauces, soups, stews, and other dishes.

Products like these are known as food analogs, natural-food look-alikes that are different from the natural substance in both structure and origin. Imitation cheeses can be textured and flavored to taste like cream cheese, American cheese, mozzarella, Parmesan, and many other varieties. They can be found in cheeseburgers, cheese sandwiches, cheese sauces, Mexican food, cheese snacks and spreads, and in ordinary-looking slices and cubes served in restaurants, school cafeterias, and other institutional dining facilities.

Ice cream, baked goods, and candy bars may be chock full of "pecans," "walnuts," and "almonds" that are really defatted peanuts, chemically treated and artifically flavored to resemble the costlier nuts. The maraschino "cherry" on top of your ice cream sundae may very well be a processed, artifically colored grape, and the blueberry "buds" in that package of frozen waffles aren't buds from a blueberry bush but tiny, chemically formed solids derived from a sugary blue syrup that may or may not be made from real blueberries.

When it comes to analogs of costly protein foods like meat, the food processors present their new achievements with real pride. Most of us are already familiar with imitation bacon bits. Made from soybeans, vegetable oil, and artificial flavoring and coloring, these crunchy morsels keep indefinitely and can be sprinkled on salads or sandwiches, or into egg dishes. But today's foodmakers also give us other meatless meat analogs made by a sophisticated process in which soybeans are spun into a chewy mass called textured soy protein, or textured vegetable protein (TVP). The meatlike fibers can be colored and flavored to simulate bacon strips, ham, chicken, and turkey, and are also used to make frankfurters, as well as bologna and other lunch meats. So far the most widespread use of TVP has been as a meat extender that can be added to hamburger. But already processors have come up with a TVP "steak," its charred-looking surface crisscrossed with artificial grill marks.

Artificial eggs have, of course, been on the market for some time in the form of low-cholesterol Egg Beaters. These come in frozen-liquid form and are really yolkless eggs that in addition to the natural whites, contain vegetable oil, nonfat dry milk, lecithin, and artificial flavor and color. People who read the label before they buy this product know they are getting an egg with an imitation yolk that lacks many of the nutrients of whole eggs, and that can't be used for much besides scrambled eggs. But the next time you order a sliced-egg sandwich in a luncheonette you might, without knowing it, be getting both an imitation yolk *and* white, sliced from a foot-long "hard-cooked egg replacement" that never saw the inside of an eggshell.

The food processors make no apologies for these deceptions. On the contrary, they proclaim them as beneficial to health (because they can reduce cholesterol and saturated-fat intake) and as a boon to the human race because soy protein can thus be introduced into the diets of the protein-hungry poor. The makers of these new products also point out that ham, bacon, and shellfish analogs add flavor and variety to the diets of people whose religion forbids the eating of pork and/or certain types of seafood.

But how sound are these claims? TVP, because of its intensive processing, is far too costly to help feed the populations of poor nations. And artificially flavored and colored foods are hardly a nutritional bargain for anyone. For the food industry, however, analogs may well be the highest profit item yet, the bonanza of the future unless consumers make it a point to assess them carefully and knowledgeably while they are still in their infancy.

SUPERMARKET TRAPS

Another area where the consumer needs to tread with care is along the well-stocked aisles of today's supermarkets. Studies show that impulse buying—the purchase of items you did not plan on getting when you entered the store—accounts for up to 70 percent of supermarket sales.

Then there are the advertised specials, the sale items that drew us into the store in the first place. These are known as "loss leaders," and the reason the store can afford to offer them at reduced prices is that almost nobody leaves without buying a good many other items as well. Even when the loss leader is depleted, the disappointed shopper who has been hooked by the bait of the advertised special, frequently buys *something* once inside the supermarket. Comparatively few shoppers ask for "rain checks," so that they can buy the product at the special price at a later date, and even fewer customers use them.

Long in advance of our visit, the supermarket planners have mapped out the traffic patterns we will follow as we walk around the store. Shelf displays have been set up accordingly, with the big food companies usually acquiring the best locations, designed to attract the attention at eye level in the best-lighted and most-frequented aisles. Small impulse items like candy and gum are, of course, displayed near the checkout lines to catch the eye of impatient adults and clamoring children.

Foods that the supermarket itself packages, like meats and cheeses, often trap the hurried or careless shopper. Thin-sliced pork chops may be priced higher per pound than medium-sliced chops; chicken thighs or chicken drumsticks may cost more per pound than whole chicken legs (which are easy to disjoint at home). And, of course, quartered chickens are more expensive than whole chickens.

The wheel of cheese that is cut up and plastic-wrapped behind the scenes in the dairy or deli department may be put out for sale at three or four different prices, depending on whether the cheese is offered as wedges, slices, grated cheese, or "cocktail cubes." The latter two, which help to use up all the curved edges and odd-sized leftovers of the wheel, are usually tagged at the highest prices per pound.

Supermarkets that package fruit and vegetable items are really denying the shopper the right to buy the quantity, quality, and size of apples, lemons, green peppers, or tomatoes that he or she wants. At the same time, the store adds on the cost of the packaging materials and labor. Stores should always provide a customer-use scale for weighing such packaged food so the shopper can make sure the weight marked on the wrapping is correct. Unfortunately, when it comes to foisting short weight, inferior quality, rotted produce, and spoiled meats on consumers, supermarkets in poor neighborhoods have almost always been found to be the worst offenders.

NO FRILLS OR MORE FRILLS?

As the price of food climbs ever higher, some supermarkets have found themselves in financial trouble, unable to meet the competition of other better-managed or better-patronized stores. Major factors in thinning supermarket profits have also been the popularity of the fast-food chains, where Americans spend more and more of their food dollars, the declining national birthrate, and the soaring costs of in-store labor and energy. Frozen food departments alone can nowadays account for up to 50 percent of a food market's energy bill.

As a result, some of the nation's largest chains were forced into bankruptcy during the late 1970s, and a new trend in supermarkets began to appear. Known as "no-frills" stores, the first of these "unsuper" markets was a branch of a West German chain that was opened in Burlington, Iowa, in 1976. On the theory that supermarket customers are tired of paying, via hidden food costs, for everything from the electronic doors to the paper bags, no-frills markets are designed to pare overhead costs to the minimum.

Most offer only about 500 nonperishable items—no meats, eggs, dairy products, produce, or frozen foods—and display them in open cartons, warehouse fashion, under bare fluorescent bulbs. Customers bring their own bags or boxes, choose from a modest variety of name brands, pay cash on the line, and do their own grocery packing. Studies so far show that consumers can save as much as 30 percent on their weekly food bill by shopping for staples at one of the stripped-down warehouse-type supermarkets, and although there were only about a thousand no-frills markets nationwide by 1980, the trend may very well continue.

At the opposite extreme, some food retailers feel that the way to win back customers is to offer *more* frills—sleeker, more attractive stores with carpeted aisles and hanging plants, in-store cocktail lounges and fast food eateries, special service departments where customers can order new eyeglasses, have their teeth checked, or their hair done, and most of all computerized shopping services that presumably save time though not necessarily money.

Already some supermarkets offer computer-operated telephone and drive-in shopping that the customer can do without leaving home or car. And since the late 1960s, it has been possible for stores to install electronic optical scanners that can add up purchases at the checkout counter instead of the clerk's having to ring up the price of each item on the cash register.

The key to this technological development, known as computerized supermarket checkout, is the Universal Product Code (UPC), a symbol made up of closely spaced lines, bars, and numbers that appears on almost all the cans, boxes, and other food containers we buy today. In a store equipped with this electronic system, the checkout clerk need only slide the UPC symbol across the scanning device in order to record on a readout screen the name and the price of the product.

The 750 to 1,000 supermarkets across the country that are now using this expensive new technology claim that it saves money in the long run. By not having to stamp a price on every item in the store, labor costs are reduced. This saving, supermarket executives say, will eventually be passed on to the customer. They also claim there is greater speed and accuracy with computerized checkout.

But consumer organizations, like the Consumer Federation of America, don't agree. Computers, they point out, can make mistakes, too. And, as far as speed is concerned, the fact that computerizing each checkout lane costs the store at least $15,000 may actually lead to fewer and longer checkout lines. But most serious, consumer groups feel, is the absence of individual prices on each item in the store.

Prices do appear on the shelf rim under the item, and some computer receipts show a printout of the product name alongside the price paid. But foods not stamped with prices tend to leave the shopper in the dark for purposes of comparison. Unpriced items also give stores the opportunity to program their computers with higher prices than those noted on the store shelves. Lastly, even if stores do play fair on prices, can they be counted on to pass on to their customers the presumed savings rather than the monstrous cost of the computerizing itself?

WHAT CONSUMERS WANT

What America's food shoppers really want, according to public hearings held in the late 1970s by the Food and Drug Administration, the United States Department of Agriculture, and the Federal Trade Commission, is *not* more electronic frills from the supermarket chains or more "taste thrills" from the food industry. They want, with the help of the government agencies involved, better labeling, more truth in advertising, and a meaningful dating system by which to judge the freshness of foods.

Among the special peeves of consumers are labels that read "vegetable shortening" without saying what kind, "standard of identity" foods like butter, ketchup, and mayonnaise that aren't required by law to reveal the presence of additives like artificial coloring and MSG, and pre-sweetened cereals that don't tell what percentage of sugar they contain.

Consumers also object to vague and misleading terms like "pure" and "natural," and they want some kind of action on fortified processed foods that manufacturers try to pass off as more nutritious than whole foods, such as the much advertised orange juice substitutes that contain sweeteners, synthetic vitamins and minerals, coloring, and other artificial substances.

Very confusing to most shoppers are the Recommended Daily Allowances listed on many food labels. The RDAs were first established in the 1940s by the Food and Nutrition Board of the National Academy of Sciences-National Research Council, which despite its official-sounding name is not a government agency. Nevertheless the Food and Nutrition Board's RDAs have FDA approval and have appeared since 1976 on the labels of products that claim nutritional merit to show what proportions of the various nutrients may be found in the product.

This labeling feature looks good on the surface. However RDA requirements, which are reexamined every five or six years, have always tended to be considerably higher than those of other nutrition authorities, like the World Health Organization (WHO).

The processed-food industry goes along with the generous RDA margins by adding impressively large amounts of synthetic vitamins and minerals to such products as pre-sweetened cereals, for the cost to the manufacturer is small. Although touted as highly nutritious, such products may actually be of low nutritional merit because they do not contain other important nutrients and are loaded with sugar and artificial flavorings, colorings, and preservatives.

Whole foods, on the other hand, which do not carry RDA listings but usually are nutritionally superior, may be bypassed by the food shopper who places too much confidence in the RDA percentages on processed-food labels.

While the food industry argues that the more specific ingredient labeling that the public wants will increase food costs (which it will then be forced to pass on to the consumer) advertising continues to be one of the industry's major expenditures. Nearly 30 percent of all the money spent on TV advertising is spent by the food industry. And most of that money goes for the promotion of nonnutritious beverages, sweets, fats and oils, baked goods, snack foods, and the limited menus of the fast food chains.

The American public depends on television advertising for most of its nutrition information, but the picture that is presented is distinctly one-sided. Young children, low-income consumers, and the elderly are probably the most taken in by the murky but important-sounding claims for junk foods that provide "more food energy" (which in ordinary language means more calories) and that are touted as being packed with nutrition. This audience is the least likely to seek out reliable nutrition information from books, magazines, newspapers, or the pamphlets and programs of government or consumer agencies.

Labels that don't tell the whole story and advertising that is deliberately misleading aren't the only food-industry abuses that bring consumer complaints. One of the most baffling bits of information stamped or printed on a bottle, can, jar, or other food container is the date.

Presumably, dating a carton of milk, a pound of butter, a loaf of bread, or a jar of mayonnaise is a way of letting the supermarket staff and the shopper know how fresh the food is and how much shelf life it can be expected to have. But, as no uniform dating system has ever been established, dates (when they aren't written in a secret code that only the manufacturer understands) are baffling at best. Unless there is an explanation preceding the date, such as "sell by . . ." or "not to be used after . . . ," it's hard for the consumer to know if the date means the day of manufacture, the day the food left the plant, the last day for sale, or the last day to be eaten.

Some shoppers try to beat the system—if such a confused state of affairs can be called a system—by simply choosing the product with the most recent date on it. But even this method isn't foolproof. How, for example, can one be sure that items haven't been postdated at the plant, so that even next month's butter is already rancid, or that the milk dated four days hence hasn't already spent half a day sitting in the hot sun out back of the supermarket?

In a distribution and marketing system as far-flung and as complex as ours, consumers need all the help they can get to preserve access to good nutrition, variety, freshness, flavor, and value in their food choices.

We can show our preferences, first of all, through our selection of foods, but also through individual and group action. We can and should make our complaints known to food retailers, food manufacturers, and to the local, state, and federal agencies concerned with consumer protection, as well as to our congressional and other government representatives.

The addresses of local consumer assistance agencies can usually be found in the telephone book. Here are a few addresses in the nation's capital to which we can write for help:

Special Assistant to the President for Consumer Affairs
The White House
Washington, D.C. 20501

Food and Drug Administration
Washington, D.C. 20204
   (*complaints about labeling and food quality*)

Federal Trade Commission
Washington, D.C. 20580
   (*complaints about false advertising claims*)

Superintendent of Documents
United States Government Printing Office
Washington, D.C. 20402
   (*reliable food and nutrition information in inexpensive pamphlet
      form*)

Center for Science in the Public Interest
1755 S Street N.W.
Washington, D.C. 20009
   (*reliable food and nutrition information in inexpensive book,
      booklet, and poster form*)

PART
3

NATURAL
FOOD
RECIPES
FOR NOW

METRIC CONVERSION TABLE

The amounts of the ingredients
called for in the recipes in this book
can be converted to metric units as
follows:

VOLUME

1 teaspoon = 5 milliliters
1 tablespoon = 15 milliliters
1 fluid ounce = 30 milliliters
1 cup = 0.24 liter
1 pint = 0.47 liter
1 quart = 0.95 liter
(to convert liters to quarts,
multiply by 1.06)

WEIGHT

1 ounce = 28 grams
3½ ounces = 100 grams
4 ounces = 114 grams
8 ounces = 227 grams
1 pound = 0.45 kilogram
2.2 pounds = 1 kilogram
(to convert grams to ounces,
multiply by .035)

After reading about the poor food choices that so many Americans make and the many nutritional deceptions practiced by the food industry, the question that naturally pops to mind is, "What is there left to eat?"

Happily the answer is, "Plenty!"

The guidelines for a good diet, using foods that are as close as possible to their natural state, are so simple that they can be reduced to four basic groups. Our daily menus should include some selections from each of the following categories:

1. *Milk and milk products*, including cheese, yogurt, and butter. Except for butter and cream, which are mostly fat but rich in vitamins A and D, the foods in this group provide a complete protein, calcium and most other important minerals (except iron), and vitamins A and D plus the B vitamins.

2. *Meats and other protein sources*, including poultry, fish, eggs, legumes, nuts, and seeds. This group provides protein in complete form from a single animal food (or from a combination of complementary plant sources) as well as iron, the B vitamins, and vitamin E.

3. *Vegetables and fruits*, including citrus fruits and juices, and vegetable oils. This group provides fiber, minerals, vitamins A, C, and E, and the B vitamins.

4. *Grains*, including whole-grain cereals, breads, macaroni, and rice whenever possible. This group provides a complete protein when grains are combined with complementary plant foods, as well as high-quality carbohydrates, iron, fiber, the B vitamins, and vitamin E.

The aim of the recipes that follow is to show how to prepare these foods by simple, healthful cooking techniques that emphasize natural flavors and the preservation of nutrients. No heavily processed foods are used in the recipes, and even lightly processed, canned or frozen foods are used very sparingly. Both traditional and newer dishes will be found, as well as ethnic contributions from many parts of the world.

Cooking from scratch may sound like a lot more work than using "convenience" foods. But just think of the energy, in the form of cooking fuel, and the long time it takes for a TV dinner—with its ragged meat, gluey gravy, rubbery vegetables, and sugary dessert—to emerge from the oven. Putting together your own meals is fun, creative, and fulfilling, as well as cheaper and far more nutritious. It can also be time-saving, for soups, casseroles, breads, and desserts may easily be made up in larger quantities in a single cooking operation. They can then be stretched over several meals, with alternate menus served on the days in between.

Most of all, cooking can and should be a family project in which all family members plan, shop for, and help prepare the meals. And because food is the center of life, families—especially in today's busy eat-and-run era—should try to eat together whenever possible, giving mealtime the dignity it deserves and making it an occasion for pleasant informality and relaxed conversation.

Perhaps we can, after all, blend the deliciously wholesome home-cooked meals and the healthy family patterns of the past with the best that twentieth-century America has to offer.

APPLE-ORANGE QUENCHER

For a refreshing natural fruit drink at any time of day, combine equal parts of chilled orange juice and apple juice (unfiltered and preservative-free). Add a squeeze of lemon or lime.

Delicious variations using either or both juices can be made by adding ripe mashed banana, mashed fresh strawberries, or other fruits, alone or in combination. Use ½ to ¾ cup of mashed fruit to 1 cup of juice. Whiz in the blender or shake well in a tightly capped jar with a little crushed ice. If you wish, flavor with a dash of vanilla extract or cinnamon. For a sweeter drink, add a little honey to taste.

YOGURT DIP FOR RAW VEGETABLES

½ cup farmer cheese or dry pot cheese (4 ounces)
⅓ cup yogurt
4 tablespoons mayonnaise
½ small clove garlic, put through garlic press (optional)
¼ cup finely chopped walnuts
½ teaspoon lemon juice
1 tablespoon finely cut fresh parsley
salt and freshly ground black pepper to taste

In a medium-size bowl, mash cheese. Blend in yogurt and mayonnaise. Add remaining ingredients and check seasoning to taste. Cover bowl and refrigerate at least 2 hours before serving. Makes about 1 cup dip.

Serve dip sprinkled with a little extra finely cut parsley or finely chopped walnuts. Raw vegetables to be dipped may include celery sticks, carrot sticks, cucumber or zucchini slices (with well-scrubbed skins left on), green or red pepper strips, radishes, whole cherry tomatoes, cauliflowerets, etc. Yogurt dip may also be served with whole-grain crackers or with firm whole-grain bread cut into squares or triangles.

EGGPLANT "CAVIAR"

1 large eggplant or 2 small eggplants (1½ pounds total)
3 tablespoons oil, preferably olive oil or sesame oil
1 medium-size onion, finely diced
1 clove garlic, put through garlic press
1 medium-size green pepper, cut in very small dice
1 tablespoon finely cut fresh parsley
¼ teaspoon salt
freshly ground black pepper
1 tablespoon lemon juice

Heat oven to 375 degrees. Wash but do not skin eggplant. Place it on a shallow pan and bake for 45 minutes, or until soft throughout. While eggplant is baking, heat 2 tablespoons of the oil in a deep-sided 9- or 10-inch skillet. Add onion, garlic, and green pepper, and cook covered over low heat until vegetables are tender but not brown.

Remove skin from baked eggplant, cut it into cubes, and

add to skillet along with parsley, salt, and a pinch or two of black pepper, to taste. Cover skillet and cook over low heat for 10 minutes. Mash contents well, add the lemon juice and the remaining tablespoon of oil.

Adjust seasoning to taste, cool, and chill. Serve as an appetizer with Middle Eastern-type "pita" or "pocket" bread (whole wheat, if possible) that has been warmed in the oven, or with whole-grain crackers or bread. Makes 1½ to 2 cups.

COLD CUCUMBER-WALNUT SOUP

4 large-size cucumbers
2 cups yogurt (1 pint)
1 cup sour cream
3 tablespoons olive oil
1 clove garlic, put through garlic press
1½ teaspoons salt
1 teaspoon finely cut chives
¼ teaspoon crumbled oregano or finely cut mint leaves
finely chopped walnuts

Pare cucumbers. Cut into spears lengthwise and remove any large, tough seeds. Cut spears crosswise into thin slices. Add all remaining ingredients except walnuts. Whirl in a blender or beat vigorously with an egg beater. Adjust seasoning to taste. Chill and serve very cold, topping each serving with finely chopped walnuts. Makes 6 to 8 servings.

SPLIT-PEA AND CARROT SOUP

1¼ cups dried green or yellow split-peas (about ½ pound)
5½ cups water
1 large onion, cut in large pieces
2 large carrots, pared or well-scrubbed, and cut in 1-inch chunks
3 ribs celery, cut in 1-inch chunks
3 to 4 sprigs celery tops
3 to 4 sprigs parsley
4 whole cloves
1 bay leaf
3 teaspoons salt
1 teaspoon dry English mustard, or other sharp-flavored mustard

Wash split-peas in a strainer and pick over. In a 4-quart soup pot, combine all ingredients except salt and mustard. Cover, bring to a boil, lower heat to simmering, and cook covered 2 hours.

Remove cloves and bay leaf. Add salt and mustard. Whirl soup in blender in several batches until smooth, or put soup mixture through a coarse strainer and return the mashed contents of the strainer to the soup. Adjust seasoning to taste. Heat through to serve. Makes 5 to 6 servings.
Note: Whole-grain bread or rolls make a hearty accompaniment to this soup. Also, the split-peas and the grain will complement each other to provide a complete protein.

LENTIL AND ZUCCHINI SOUP

1 ¼ cups dried lentils, washed in a strainer and picked over
6 ½ cups water
1 medium-large onion, cut in ¼-inch dice
2 cloves garlic, put through garlic press
2 medium-large zucchini with skins, well-scrubbed, and cut in
*   ½-inch dice*
1 rib celery, cut in ¼-inch dice
1 carrot, cut in ¼-inch dice
3 to 4 sprigs celery tops
3 to 4 sprigs parsley
2 teaspoons salt
⅛ teaspoon freshly ground black pepper
¼ teaspoon each oregano, basil, and mint

In a 4-quart soup pot combine all ingredients except the salt, pepper, and herbs. Cover, bring to a boil, lower heat to simmering, and cook covered 2 hours. Add remaining ingredients.

Put about 1 cup of the soup mixture through a coarse strainer, returning strained mixture to the soup but discarding the lentil skins left in the strainer. This will give the soup a thicker base. Adjust seasoning to taste. Heat through to serve. Makes 6 to 8 servings. *Note:* Try chunks of whole-wheat Italian bread with the soup. The lentils and the grain will complement each other to provide a complete protein.

EGGPLANT AND MOZZARELLA BAKE

3 ½ cups tomato sauce (see recipe below)
1 eggplant, 1 ½ to 1 ¾ pounds
salt
oil (safflower, corn, or other polyunsaturated type)
½ cup freshly grated Parmesan cheese
½ pound mozzarella cheese, cut in slices ⅛-inch thick

TOMATO SAUCE

2 tablespoons olive oil
2 medium-size onions, cut in ¼-inch dice
2 small cloves garlic, put through garlic press
1 medium-size green pepper, cut in ¼-inch dice
1 2-pound, 3-ounce can Italian-style plum tomatoes
2 tablespoons tomato paste
½ teaspoon dried basil leaves
½ teaspoon dried oregano leaves
2 teaspoons salt
¼ teaspoon freshly ground black pepper
1 teaspoon honey
2 tablespoons finely cut fresh parsley, or 2 teaspoons dried parsley
1 large bay leaf

Heat olive oil in a deep, heavy-bottomed 10-inch skillet. Add onion, garlic, and green pepper, and stir them in the hot oil with a wooden spoon for 3 minutes. Lower heat and add all remaining ingredients. Reduce heat to very low and simmer uncovered for 1½ hours. Stir occasionally while cooking. Makes about 3½ cups sauce, which may also be used with spaghetti or other pasta. (For a meat sauce, add ¾ pound lean ground beef along with onion and stir until it loses its red color. Proceed as directed.)

To prepare eggplant and mozzarella dish, remove skin from eggplant with a vegetable parer or a sharp knife. Wash eggplant and cut it crosswise into slices ¼-inch thick. Arrange slices, slightly overlapping, on a large shallow pan, sprinkle lightly with salt and drizzle with oil. Broil 5 minutes or until light brown. Turn slices, repeat salt and oil, and broil 5 minutes more or until just tender. Repeat until all eggplant is broiled.

Set oven to heat to 350 degrees. Lightly butter or oil a 9x13x2 baking dish. Spoon one-fourth of the tomato sauce on the bottom. Arrange half the broiled eggplant slices atop sauce. Sprinkle with one-third of the grated Parmesan cheese. Add another fourth of the sauce, and arrange half the slices of mozzarella on top. Repeat, using another fourth of the sauce, rest of eggplant, and another third of the Parmesan cheese. Top with remaining fourth of sauce, rest of mozzarella slices, and sprinkle with the final third of the Parmesan cheese.

Bake at 350 degrees for 30 minutes, or until cheese begins to be very lightly browned at top. Let dish stand at room temperature for about 5 minutes. Serve directly from baking dish. Makes 6 to 8 servings as a main course with bread and a salad.

TOASTED CHEESE PUFF

12 slices enriched firm-type white bread, or use half white bread and half whole-wheat bread
butter or margarine
2½ cups coarsely shredded sharp Cheddar cheese (about ⅝ pound)
4 eggs
1½ teaspoons salt
½ teaspoon paprika
½ teaspoon dry English mustard, or other sharp-flavored mustard
1 teaspoon Worcestershire sauce
3 drops Tabasco sauce
2 cups milk

Cut off crusts of bread, and butter each slice. (Save crusts to be dried and crushed for use in recipes calling for dried bread crumbs.) Butter a 2-quart casserole or deep baking dish. Cut each slice of bread into 4 triangles and arrange in a single layer to cover bottom of baking dish. Cut and shape pieces where necessary to fit bread in snugly. Sprinkle with a layer of the shredded cheese. Repeat until all the bread and cheese have been used up, making about 4 layers of each.

In a bowl beat eggs, add seasonings and milk. Pour evenly over contents of baking dish. Cover dish and store in refrigerator for at least 4 hours, or overnight.

To bake cheese puff, set oven to heat to 350 degrees. Bake, uncovered, 40 to 50 minutes, or until puffed and deep golden brown on top. Serve hot, directly from baking dish. Sliced tomatoes or a tossed salad are a good accompaniment. Makes 6 to 8 servings.

SPINACH PIE

1 9-inch pie shell, preferably whole-wheat pastry

WHOLE WHEAT PASTRY

½ cup whole wheat flour, unsifted
½ cup unbleached white flour, sifted
¼ teaspoon salt
⅓ cup butter (or use half margarine)
3 to 4 tablespoons beaten whole egg

In a medium-size mixing bowl, combine flours and salt. Cut in butter with a pastry blender, or with two knives worked crisscross fashion, until the shortening is the size of coarse bread crumbs. Add the egg, a tablespoon at a time, stirring with a fork so that moisture is evenly distributed. Mix vigorously until large clumps are formed. Then gather the dough into a ball with your fingers.

Place dough on a floured board or pastry cloth, flatten it slightly, and roll with a floured rolling pin into a circle about 11 inches in diameter. Fit pastry loosely into a 9-inch pie plate. With floured fingers, form a standing rim of dough and pinch or flute the rim as desired. Chill pie shell in refrigerator while preparing filling.

SPINACH FILLING

1 tablespoon butter
1 medium-size onion, cut in ¼-inch dice
1 small clove garlic, put through garlic press

*1 10-ounce package frozen chopped spinach, cooked and drained, or
    use 1 pound fresh spinach, cooked, drained, and chopped*
2 tablespoons butter, melted
1 cup grated Swiss cheese
¼ cup grated Parmesan cheese
¾ cup yogurt
3 eggs, beaten
¾ teaspoon salt
⅛ teaspoon white pepper
⅛ teaspoon nutmeg

Set oven to heat to 375 degrees. Heat the 1 tablespoon of
butter in a small skillet and gently fry onion and garlic until
very light brown. Add to the hot, cooked spinach. Add the
2 tablespoons melted butter and all the remaining ingredients.

Turn mixture into pastry shell. Place a large flat pan on
the oven shelf beneath the pie to catch any drippings. Bake
spinach pie at 375 degrees for 40 minutes, or until center is
mounded and firm. Cool for 5 to 10 minutes. Serve in
wedges, while still warm, with a mixed salad. Makes 6 to 8
servings as a main course.

POTATO CHEESE PANCAKES

1 8-ounce package cream cheese, softened at room temperature
2 eggs
4 cups finely grated raw potato (drained of excess liquid)
½ cup coarsely shredded Swiss cheese
1 small onion, finely grated
1½ teaspoons salt
¼ teaspoon white pepper

2 tablespoons dried bread crumbs
oil for frying (safflower, corn, or other polyunsaturated type)

In a large mixing bowl, mash cream cheese with the back of a wooden spoon. Add eggs one at a time and beat well with a wire whisk. Add grated potato and all remaining ingredients, except oil.

Cover bottom of a 10-inch, deep-sided frying pan with oil to a depth of ⅛-inch. Heat until a few drops of water sprinkled on oil cause it to sputter gently. Drop potato mixture from a large spoon to form oval mounds 3½ to 4 inches long, five or six to the pan.

When pancakes are well browned on bottom, turn and fry other side. Remove and place on paper toweling to drain off excess oil. Fry the rest of the pancakes, adding oil to the pan as necessary. Serve potato cheese pancakes hot, with chilled yogurt and applesauce. Makes 24 to 28 pancakes.

Note: These pancakes make a good main course because the potatoes and the cheeses combine to provide a complete protein.

FRIED BROWN RICE WITH MUSHROOMS

peanut oil (about ⅓ cup total)
1 clove garlic, put through garlic press
¾ cup celery, cut in ⅛-inch slices
¾ cup scallions, white part only, cut in ¼-inch slices
salt
⅓ cup raw peanuts (unroasted, no oil or salt added)
2 cups sliced fresh mushrooms (washed but not peeled)
¾ cup green parts of scallions, cut in ¼-inch pieces

¾ cup brown rice, uncooked
2 cups water
1 egg
soy sauce (preferably preservative-free type)

In a deep 10-inch skillet that has a cover, heat 1½ tablespoons of the peanut oil. Add garlic, celery, and white parts of scallions, sprinkle with a little salt, and stir-fry with a wooden spoon until the vegetables are beginning to get tender but are still crisp. Remove with a slotted spoon and set aside in a bowl.

Add 1 tablespoon of peanut oil to the skillet. Add peanuts and stir-fry until very pale golden-brown. Remove with a slotted spoon to a separate bowl. Add another tablespoon of peanut oil, add mushrooms and green parts of scallions, sprinkle with a little salt, and stir-fry just until beginning to get limp. Remove and add to the bowl containing the other vegetables.

Now add a tablespoon of oil to the hot skillet and the brown rice, which has been rinsed in a strainer. Stir rice grains until translucent, lower heat, and add the 2 cups of water and ½ teaspoon of salt. Cover skillet tightly and cook rice about one hour, or until it is tender and all the water is absorbed.

While rice is finishing cooking, heat an 8-inch frying pan, cover bottom with a little peanut oil, and when oil is hot add egg which has been well beaten with a teaspoon of water and a pinch of salt. Fry egg on both sides to make a very thin omelet. Remove to a plate and slice into long shreds, about ¼-inch wide.

Gently fold vegetables, peanuts, and omelet slices into hot cooked brown rice. Heat through very gently and season to taste with soy sauce. Serve with a cooked vegetable such as fresh broccoli. Makes 4 servings as a main course.

TORTILLAS WITH REFRIED BEANS

1 cup pink or pinto beans, washed, picked over, and drained
1 medium-size onion, coarsely diced
1 quart cold water
1 teaspoon salt
¼ teaspoon chili powder
4 tablespoons oil (corn, safflower, or other polyunsaturated type)
1 clove garlic, put through garlic press
1 medium-size onion, cut in ¼-inch dice
1 small green pepper, cut in ¼-inch dice
1 medium-size tomato, cut in ½-inch dice
8 to 9 tortillas, about 5 inches in diameter (canned are acceptable)
oil for frying tortillas
1¼ cups coarsely shredded sharp Cheddar cheese
3 ripe tomatoes, cut in large cubes
1½ cups crisp shredded lettuce
oil-and-vinegar salad dressing, optional (may use salad dressing
*   recipe given for* Raw Spinach Salad)

Combine beans, the coarsely diced onion, and water in a 4-quart pot. Cover, bring to a boil, reduce heat, and simmer for 2 to 2½ hours, or until beans are very tender. Drain beans. Add salt and chili powder to beans and mash entire mixture.

In a deep 9- or 10-inch skillet, heat 2 tablespoons of the oil. Add garlic, onion, and green pepper. Fry until tender. Add diced tomato and fry a few more minutes. Sprinkle lightly with a little additional salt and chili powder.

Add the remaining 2 tablespoons of the oil to the skillet. When it is hot, add the mashed bean mixture and blend in with the vegetables. Fry just until bean mash is becoming crusty on the bottom. Turn with a spatula and fry other side. Turn off heat and cover skillet to keep refried beans warm.

In another skillet, heat just enough oil to cover bottom. Add tortillas, a layer at a time, and fry about one-half minute on each side. Tortillas should not be fried completly crisp.

Place tortillas on paper toweling to drain excess oil. Then spread each tortilla with hot bean mixture, sprinkle with about 2½ tablespoons of the grated cheese, and top with cubed tomato and shredded lettuce that has been mixed with oil-and-vinegar salad dressing. Tortillas can be eaten in the hand. Makes 3 to 4 servings.

Note: The tortillas—which are made from corn—and the beans combne to provide a complete protein.

PASTITSIO
(A Greek macaroni, meat, and cheese dish)

MACARONI MIXTURE

3 quarts water
1 tablespoon oil
2 teaspoons salt
½ pound small elbow macaroni
2 tablespoons butter or margarine
½ teaspoon salt
⅓ cup beaten egg
2 tablespoons grated kefalotyri *or Parmesan cheese*

WHITE SAUCE MIXTURE

3 tablespoons butter or margarine
6 tablespoons flour
2 cups milk
1 teaspoon salt
⅓ cup beaten egg
2 tablespoons grated kefalotyri *or Parmesan cheese*

MEAT MIXTURE

1 tablespoon butter or margarine
1 onion, cut in ¼-inch dice
1 pound ground lean lamb or beef
4 drained canned tomatoes or 4 fresh ripe tomatoes, cut up
¾ teaspoon salt
¼ teaspoon cinnamon
⅛ teaspoon freshly ground black pepper
2 tablespoons dried bread crumbs
½ cup grated kefalotyri *or Parmesan cheese*

To prepare the macaroni mixture, place the water, oil, and 2 teaspoons of salt in a 6-quart pot. Cover, bring to a boil, add macaroni, and cook at a boil until elbows are tender, about 12 to 15 minutes. Stir frequently to prevent sticking. Pour water and elbows into a colander or large strainer. Rinse elbows with cold water and drain well. In the still-warm pot in which the macaroni was cooked, melt the butter. Remove pot from heat and add the drained macaroni, the ½ teaspoon salt, ⅓ cup beaten egg, and the 2 tablespoons of grated cheese. Cover and set aside.

To prepare the white sauce, melt the butter or margarine in a medium-size saucepan. Measure flour into a bowl, add cold milk a little at a time, and beat with a wire whisk to form a smooth mixture. Add to the melted butter and stir constantly over medium heat until mixture is thickened. Beat occasionally with whisk to prevent lumpiness. Cool mixture. Add the salt, beaten egg, and grated cheese. Cover and set aside.

To prepare meat mixture, melt butter or margarine in a deep 9- or 10-inch skillet. Add onion and cook until lightly browned. Add meat in small clumps and cook, stirring with a wooden spoon, until it loses its pink color. Add tomatoes, salt, cinnamon, black pepper, and dried bread crumbs.

Set oven to heat to 350 degrees. To assemble pastitsio, lightly butter a 9x9x2 baking pan. Add half the macaroni mixture. Sprinkle with some of the ½ cup of grated cheese. Add half the meat mixture, sprinkle with more grated cheese, add half the white sauce, and sprinkle with a little more grated cheese. Repeat, using up all of the grated cheese. Bake 40 minutes or until mixture is set and beginning to turn very pale gold on top. Cool 10 to 12 minutes. Serve directly from baking dish. Makes 6 to 8 servings.

BAKED LEMON CHICKEN

2 broiler chickens (2½ to 3 pounds each), cut into 8 quarters
3 tablespoons butter, melted
3 tablespoons lemon juice
1 large clove garlic, put through garlic press
¾ teaspoon salt
⅛ teaspoon freshly ground black pepper
1 teaspoon finely cut chives
paprika

Set oven to heat to 350 degrees. Wash chicken quarters and pat dry. Break wing-bone joint so that breast quarters lie flat. Arrange chicken, skin side up, on lightly buttered foil in a shallow 10x15 baking pan. Combine all remaining ingredients except paprika. Lift chicken skin carefully away from flesh and, with a small spoon, insert lemon mixture under skin of each quarter. Spoon remaining mixture on top of chicken. Sprinkle with paprika.

Bake chicken 1¼ hours, without turning, until crisply browned on top and tender inside. Baste occasionally with liquid in pan. Makes 4 to 6 servings.

RAW SPINACH SALAD

1 pound raw spinach
thin-sliced raw mushrooms, washed but not peeled (optional)
thin-sliced raw zucchini, washed and well-scrubbed but not pared
    (optional)
coarsely chopped hard-cooked eggs (optional)
oil-and-vinegar salad dressing (see recipe below)

Wash spinach carefully to remove any sand or grit. Remove stems, drain well, and tear into large pieces. If desired add mushrooms and/or zucchini. For a main-course salad, hard-cooked eggs may be added. Keep salad greens chilled and just before serving toss lightly with enough dressing to moisten and flavor greens. Makes 6 to 8 servings.

OIL-AND-VINEGAR SALAD DRESSING

¼ cup red wine vinegar
¾ cup corn or other polyunsaturated oil (or part olive oil)
1½ teaspoons salt
¼ teaspoon freshly ground black pepper
½ teaspoon honey
½ teaspoon dry English mustard, or other sharp-flavored mustard
1 teaspoon dried oregano
1 tablespoon fresh parsley, finely cut, or 1 teaspoon dried parsley
1 clove garlic, put through garlic press
1 teaspoon grated onion

Combine all ingredients in a bowl and beat with a wire whisk. Store in refrigerator in a jar, allowing several hours for flavor to develop. Keeps for several weeks. Makes about 1 cup.

SPROUTED WHEAT AND TOMATO SALAD

1 cup sprouted wheat berries (see instructions below)
1½ tablespoons dried mint (optional)
4 tablespoons finely cut fresh parsley
2 teaspoons finely cut chives
2 tablespoons olive oil
2 tablespoons lemon juice
½ teaspoon salt
⅛ teaspoon freshly ground black pepper
4 tablespoons raw sunflower seeds, hulled
3 cups fresh tomatoes, cut in chunks

Three to four days ahead, start sprouting wheat berries (which can be purchased in health food stores). Wash and drain 4 tablespoons of wheat berries, place in a quart jar, fill jar up to two-thirds with water, and let it stand uncovered and away from bright light for from 12 to 24 hours. Then cover jar securely with cheesecloth or other porous material, turn it over, and discard water. Leave jar on its side, tipped into a bowl to drain off any remaining liquid. Twice a day, for next two days, remove cloth, fill jar with water, replace cloth, and immediately drain off water. Sprouts are ready when new growth is twice the length of the seed. Drained sprouts can then be used at once or should be stored in refrigerator for several days at most.

If using dried mint in salad, cover with boiling water and let mint steep for 10 minutes. Then drain. Combine all ingredients except tomatoes. Chill well and gently mix in tomato chunks just before serving. Makes 6 servings.

THREE BEAN SALAD

2 cups each of cooked or canned red kidney beans, chick peas, and small white beans or lentils
¾ cup celery, cut in ¼-inch dice
¾ cup green pepper, cut in ¼-inch dice
½ cup oil-and-vinegar salad dressing (see Raw Spinach Salad *recipe)*
4 tablespoons mayonnaise

To cook beans, follow method used in recipe for *Refried Beans*, adding only salt after cooking, and do not mash beans. Red kidney beans and chick peas must be soaked overnight in water to cover before cooking. Each kind of bean must be cooked separately, as cooking times will vary. Canned beans may be used instead. Turn contents into a strainer, rinse with cold water, and drain well.

Combine all beans, celery, and green pepper in a large bowl. Beat together the ½ cup oil-and-vinegar dressing and the mayonnaise. Blend into bean mixture. Taste and add salt, pepper, onion, or other seasoning if desired. Chill several hours. Makes 8 to 10 servings.

SESAME WHOLE WHEAT BREAD

1 package active dry yeast (¼ ounce), preferably preservative-free
1¼ cups lukewarm water
½ cup honey
1 cup unbleached white flour, unsifted
4 cups whole wheat flour, unsifted (approximately)
¾ cup yogurt, at room temperature
1 teaspoon salt
3 tablespoons sesame, corn, or safflower oil
¼ cup wheat germ
¼ cup sesame seeds, raw or toasted
melted butter, 2 to 3 tablespoons

In a large mixing bowl, combine yeast and lukewarm water, stirring until granules dissolve. Add honey and blend. Add white flour, 2 cups of the whole wheat flour, and the yogurt, stirring vigorously with a wooden spoon after each addition. Mixture will be loose and sticky. Cover bowl with plastic wrap and set in a warm place (such as an unheated oven, with a large pot or bowl of hot water on the shelf below) until doubled in bulk, about 1½ hours. Keep oven door closed.

Mixture will be spongy. Stir it down with a wooden spoon and add salt, oil, wheat germ, sesame seeds, and 1 more cup of whole wheat flour. Continue to add flour gradually until mixture is no longer sticky to the touch. Turn dough out onto a floured surface and knead it with the heels of your hands for 10 minutes, adding flour as needed. It should be smooth, slightly elastic, and have a dull satiny sheen at the end of the kneading period. Place dough in an oiled mixing bowl, brush top of dough lightly with oil, cover with plastic wrap, and let rise again until doubled in bulk, 1 to 1½ hours.

Punch down dough and knead one minute. Cut dough in half and shape each into a rectangle to fit into an oiled 9x5 loaf pan. Let loaves rise uncovered in a warm place until doubled, about 1 hour. Set oven heat to 350 degrees. Bake 35–40 minutes. After removing bread from oven, brush tops of hot loaves with melted butter. Cool 5 minutes and remove from pans. Makes 2 loaves.

If preferred, bake half the dough in a loaf pan and make a dozen rolls with the other half. To make cloverleaf rolls, oil a 12-cup muffin pan. Divide the remaining half of the dough into 12 parts. Roll each part into 3 equal-size balls. Dip each ball in melted butter and place 3 balls with sides touching in each muffin cup. Sprinkle with additional sesame seeds. Let rise uncovered until doubled in bulk, about 1 hour. Bake, along with loaf, in 350 degree oven, but remove rolls after 30 minutes. Brush with melted butter.

Home-baked rolls and bread keep well in the freezer. Bread may be sliced (using a serrated knife) before freezing and can be heated or toasted in a few minutes. Bread and rolls will thaw to room temperature in 15 to 20 minutes.

YOGURT ONION CORNBREAD

1 cup yellow cornmeal (including germ)
1 cup sifted unbleached white flour
3 teaspoons baking powder
½ teaspoon baking soda
1 teaspoon salt
2 eggs
⅞ cup yogurt (1 cup less 2 tablespoons)
¼ cup oil (corn or other polyunsaturated type)
2 tablespoons honey
2 tablespoons grated raw onion
3 tablespoons sweet red and/or green pepper, cut in very fine dice or
   shredded on a grater

Set oven to heat to 425 degrees. In a large mixing bowl, combine cornmeal and sifted flour which has been combined with baking powder, baking soda, and salt, and sifted again.

In another bowl beat eggs and add all remaining ingredients. Add wet mixture to dry cornmeal mixture. Stir with a wooden spoon just until blended. Turn batter into a greased 9x9x2 baking pan. Bake 20 to 25 minutes, or until cornbread is crisp on top and sides come away from pan. Cut into squares and serve warm with butter. Makes 16 pieces, about 2 inches square each.

Note: If cornbread is eaten with bean soups, bean salads, chili or other bean dishes, the cornmeal and the beans complement each other to provide a complete protein.

ZUCCHINI BREAD

1⅓ cups shredded zucchini (1 large zucchini)
¾ cup sifted unbleached flour
1½ teaspoons baking powder
¼ teaspoon salt
¾ teaspoon cinnamon
¼ teaspoon cloves
⅛ teaspoon nutmeg
½ cup whole wheat flour, unsifted
2 eggs
½ cup dark brown sugar, firmly packed
¼ cup honey
⅓ cup oil (safflower, corn, or other polyunsaturated type)
1 teaspoon vanilla extract
⅓ cup coarsely chopped raw Brazil nuts
⅓ cup coarsely chopped raw pumpkin seeds
⅓ cup dark raisins

Wash zucchini and scrub skin to remove any grit, but do not pare. Slice off ends and coarsely shred zucchini on a four-sided grater. Set aside in a strainer to allow any excess liquid to drain off. Set oven to heat to 350 degrees.

Combine white flour, baking powder, salt, cinnamon, cloves, and nutmeg. Sift into a medium-size bowl and add whole wheat flour. In a large mixing bowl, beat eggs with wire whisk, add brown sugar, honey, oil, and vanilla. Blend well with whisk. Add the flour mixture, the zucchini, Brazil nuts, pumpkin seeds, and raisins, and blend.

Turn mixture into a greased 9x5 loaf pan and bake at 350 degrees for 50 to 60 minutes, or until center is firm and springs back to the touch. The crack in the center of the bread, which is characteristic, should test dry when a cake tester is inserted. Cool on rack about 10 minutes and remove from pan. Slice when completely cooled. Makes 1 loaf.

PUMPKIN DATE BREAD

2 eggs
1 cup canned pumpkin (any leftover canned pumpkin may be frozen)
⅞ cup dark brown sugar, firmly packed (1 cup less 2 tablespoons)
⅔ cup oil (safflower, corn, or other polyunsaturated type)
1 cup sifted unbleached white flour
1½ teaspoons baking powder
¼ teaspoon salt
1¼ teaspoons cinnamon
¼ teaspoon nutmeg
¼ teaspoon ginger
¾ cup whole wheat flour, unsifted
2 tablespoons wheat germ
½ cup cut-up dates
½ cup coarsely chopped walnuts

Set oven to heat to 350 degrees. In a large mixing bowl, beat eggs with a wire whisk. Add pumpkin, brown sugar, and oil. Continue beating until well blended. Combine sifted white flour, baking powder, salt, cinnamon, nutmeg, and ginger, and sift into pumpkin mixture. Add whole wheat flour and wheat germ, and blend thoroughly. Add dates and nuts.

Turn mixture into a greased 9x5 loaf pan and bake at 350 degrees 55 to 60 minutes, or until center is firm and springs back to touch. Crack in center, which is characteristic, should test dry when a cake tester is inserted. Cool on rack about 10 minutes and remove from pan. Slice when completely cooled. Makes 1 loaf.

BANANA BREAD SQUARES

⅓ *cup butter or margarine, at room temperature*
½ *cup dark brown sugar, firmly packed*
1 egg
⅓ *cup yogurt*
¾ *cup unbleached white flour, sifted*
1 teaspoon baking powder
¼ *teaspoon salt*
½ *teaspoon cinnamon*
½ *cup whole wheat flour, unsifted*
¼ *cup rolled oats, uncooked (do not use instant-type oatmeal)*
¾ *cup mashed ripe banana (1½ to 2 bananas)*
⅓ *cup raw sunflower seeds or coarsely chopped nuts*

Set oven to heat to 350 degrees. In a large mixing bowl, cream butter or margarine with the back of a wooden spoon. Add brown sugar and continue creaming until mixture is well blended and comes away from sides of bowl. Add egg and beat well with a wire whisk. Add yogurt and blend in.

Combine white flour, baking powder, salt, and cinnamon, and sift into creamed mixture. Add whole wheat flour, rolled oats, mashed banana, and sunflower seeds. Mix just to blend. Turn into a greased 8x8x2 or 9x9x2 baking pan. Bake 30 minutes at 350 degrees or until center springs back to the touch and sides shrink away from pan.

Cut into squares and serve slightly warm, or cool, buttered or plain. Makes 16 pieces, about 2 inches square each.

APPLESAUCE OATMEAL MUFFINS

2 eggs
⅔ cup dark brown sugar, firmly packed
1 cup applesauce, home-made or canned
1 cup sifted unbleached white flour
1½ teaspoons baking powder
¼ teaspoon salt
1 teaspoon cinnamon
¼ teaspoon nutmeg
½ cup whole wheat flour, unsifted
½ cup butter or margarine, melted (¼ pound or 1 stick)
1 cup rolled oats, uncooked (do not use instant-type oatmeal)
½ cup dark raisins
¼ cup raw sunflower seeds
¼ cup walnuts, coarsely chopped

Set oven to heat to 375 degrees. In a large mixing bowl, beat eggs and brown sugar with a wire whisk. Add applesauce. Combine sifted white flour, baking powder, salt, cinnamon, and nutmeg, and sift into applesauce mixture. Add all remaining ingredients in order given. Blend just to moisten.

Oil two muffin tins (12 muffin cups each). Fill two-thirds full, tucking raisins into batter to prevent burning. Bake 25 minutes or until centers spring back to touch. Remove from pans and serve warm or cool, buttered or plain. Makes 24 medium-small muffins.

CARROT PINEAPPLE CAKE

⅔ cup sifted unbleached white flour
⅔ cup whole wheat flour, unsifted
⅞ cup dark brown sugar, firmly packed (1 cup less 2 tablespoons)
¾ teaspoon baking soda
¼ teaspoon salt
1½ teaspoons cinnamon
¾ cup finely-chopped walnuts
2 eggs
½ cup yogurt
⅓ cup oil (safflower, corn, or other polyunsaturated type)
1 teaspoon vanilla extract
½ cup finely grated raw carrot (about 2 medium-size carrots)
½ cup well-drained canned crushed pineapple, unsweetened

Set oven to heat to 350 degrees. In a large mixing bowl, combine flours, brown sugar, baking soda, salt, cinnamon, and walnuts. In a medium-size bowl, beat eggs with a wire whisk, add yogurt, oil, and vanilla, and blend thoroughly. Add to dry mixture and stir with a wooden spoon just until blended. Add carrots and pineapple.

Turn batter into a greased 9x9x2 baking pan and bake 35 minutes at 350 degrees, or until top of cake springs back to the touch and sides come away from pan. Cool thoroughly. If desired, frost cake with ½ pound cream cheese that has been softened with a little yogurt or sour cream and sweetened to taste with honey. Cut into squares or rectangles. Makes 16 to 20 pieces.

APPLE CRUNCH

1 cup unbleached white flour, unsifted
½ cup whole wheat flour, unsifted
1 cup rolled oats, uncooked (do not use instant-type oatmeal)
¾ cup dark brown sugar, firmly packed
2 tablespoons wheat germ
½ teaspoon baking powder
¼ teaspoon salt
¼ pound butter or margarine (1 stick)
6 medium-large apples (use tart, crisp variety)
½ cup dark brown sugar, firmly packed
2 tablespoons flour, white or whole wheat
½ teaspoon cinnamon
¼ teaspoon ginger
2 teaspoons lemon juice

In a large mixing bowl, combine first seven ingredients. Add the butter or margarine in chunks and cut it in with a pastry blender, or two knives worked crisscross fashion, until about the size of small peas. Then work entire mixture with the fingers until moist and crumbly. Lightly butter a 9x13x2 baking dish. Pat half the mixture firmly and evenly into the bottom of the dish. Set rest of mixture aside for the topping.

Quarter the apples. Pare and remove cores, and cut into slices ¼-inch thick. Set oven to heat to 350 degrees. Combine the ½ cup brown sugar, 2 tablespoons flour, cinnamon, and ginger. Mix through the apples and add the lemon juice. Distribute apples evenly in baking dish and cover with the topping mixture, patting it down firmly with the back of a spoon. Bake 35 to 40 minutes at 350 degrees. If apples are not yet soft, reduce heat to 325 degrees and continue baking 10 to 15 minutes longer. Serve apple crunch warm or at room temperature, cut into squares and topped with a dab of honey-sweetened yogurt or, if preferred, with frozen yogurt. Makes 8 to 10 servings.

SWEET POTATO PIE

1 9-inch pie shell, preferably whole wheat pastry (see recipe for Spinach Pie)

SWEET POTATO FILLING

2 cups mashed sweet potatoes or yams (4 to 5 medium-large potatoes, pared and cooked in lightly salted boiling water until tender)
⅓ cup honey
2 tablespoons molasses
1 tablespoon grated orange rind
½ cup milk
3 eggs, beaten
1 teaspoon cinnamon
⅛ teaspoon nutmeg
½ teaspoon salt
2 tablespoons melted butter

Prepare pastry shell and chill while preparing filling. Set oven to heat to 375 degrees. Combine all ingredients in order given and blend well. As potatoes will vary in sweetness, check flavoring adding a little more honey, molasses, or spice, as desired. Turn mixture into pie shell. Place a large pan on oven shelf beneath pie to catch any drippings. Bake pie at 375 degrees for 15 minutes. Reduce heat to 325 degrees and continue baking 45 to 50 minutes longer, or until center of pie is mounded and firm.

Serve sweet potato pie at room temperature, or chilled. Top with lightly sweetened cinnamon-flavored whipped cream, if desired. Makes 8 portions.

CAROB AND HONEY BROWNIES

½ cup butter or margarine, softened at room temperature (¼ pound or 1 stick)
½ cup dark brown sugar, firmly packed
⅓ cup honey
3 teaspoons vanilla extract
3 eggs
¾ cup sifted unbleached white flour
½ cup carob powder*
¼ teaspoon salt
⅔ cup coarsely chopped walnuts
16 walnut halves

Set oven to heat to 350 degrees. In a large bowl, cream butter or margarine with the back of a wooden spoon. Add brown sugar and continue creaming until smooth and well blended. Add honey and vanilla. Add eggs one at a time,

*Carob powder and carob chips (used as a substitute for chocolate chips) are derived from St. John's Bread, the dried seed pod of a tree that grows in southerly climates. Carob is preferred to cocoa or chocolate by health food fans because it does not contain caffeine and is naturally sweet. Carob products have a light, pleasant "chocolate-malt" flavor and can be bought in health food stores.

beating after each addition. Combine flour, carob powder, and salt, and add. Add the coarsely chopped walnuts. Turn batter into a greased 9x9x2 baking pan. Smooth the surface and arrange the walnut halves atop the batter in four rows across and down. Bake 20 to 25 minutes, or until top of cake springs back to the touch and sides come away from pan. Cool on a rack, with the pan covered with a cotton or linen tea towel to keep brownies moist as they cool. When thoroughly cooled, cut into 16 squares with a walnut half in the center of each. Makes 16 brownies, about 2 inches square.

GORP COOKIES*

¾ cup butter or margarine (⅜ pound or 1½ sticks)
½ cup dark brown sugar, firmly packed
1 egg
¾ cup unbleached white flour, sifted
½ teaspoon baking powder
¼ teaspoon salt
2 teaspoons cinnamon
½ cup molasses
¾ cup whole wheat flour, unsifted
¼ cup milk
1¼ cups rolled oats, uncooked (do not use instant-type oatmeal)
2 tablespoons sesame seeds

*Gorp is a mixture of nuts, seeds, raisins, and chocolate or carob chips that is a favorite with campers and back-packers because it is nutritious, light to carry, easy to eat on the trail, and keeps well.

½ *cup coarsely chopped raw peanuts and/or cashews (unroasted; no oil or salt added)*
½ *cup raw pumpkin seeds and/or sunflower seeds*
½ *cup dark raisins*
½ *cup chocolate chips or carob chips (see note in recipe for* Carob and Honey Brownies*)*

Allow butter or margarine to soften slightly. In a large mixing bowl, mash with the back of a wooden spoon until creamy. Blend in brown sugar. Add egg and beat well. Combine white flour, baking powder, salt, and cinnamon, and sift into mixture. Add molasses and all remaining ingredients in order given, blending well after each addition.

Set oven to heat to 350 degrees. Drop mixture from a measuring tablespoon, slightly rounded, onto lightly greased cookie sheets. Dough will be stiff and will not spread much in baking. Bake at 350 degrees for 12 minutes or until centers of cookies spring back to the touch. Transfer to racks to cool. Store in tightly covered tin, or freeze. Makes about 80 cookies.

YOGURT SUNDAE

1 cup yogurt
2 cups fresh fruit, such as ripe peaches or melon cut in chunks, whole strawberries, blueberries, or seedless grapes, or sliced banana, or any desired combination of fruits
honey or brown sugar
vanilla extract or cinnamon
nutty granola topping (see recipe for Nutty Granola*)*

Combine yogurt and fruit. Add sweetening and flavoring to taste. Serve well chilled in dessert dishes topped with nutty granola. Makes about 4 servings.

NUTTY GRANOLA

2 *cups rolled oats, uncooked (do not use instant-type oatmeal)*
¼ *cup wheat germ*
¼ *cup raw unblanched almonds and/or raw Brazil nuts, coarsely chopped*
¼ *cup raw cashew nuts and/or walnuts, coarsely chopped*
¼ *cup raw pumpkin seeds (unroasted, unsalted), coarsely chopped or whole*
¼ *cup raw sunflower seeds, whole*
⅛ *cup sesame seeds*
¼ *cup raw peanuts (unroasted, unsalted), coarsely chopped*
2 *tablespoons oil (safflower, corn, or other polyunsaturated type)*
4 *tablespoons honey*
2 *teaspoons vanilla extract*
½ *cup dark raisins*

In a medium-large bowl, combine rolled oats, wheat germ, nuts, seeds, and peanuts. In a small bowl mix together the oil, honey, and vanilla extract. Add to dry mixture and blend thoroughly.

Set oven to heat to 325 degrees. Oil a large baking sheet or very shallow pan and spread out granola in a thin layer. Bake for about 12 minutes or until toasted a golden-brown, stirring mixture with a wooden spoon every 3 or 4 minutes for an even browning.

Immediately after removing granola from oven, add raisins and mix through. Cool thoroughly. Store in a tightly covered jar. Makes about 4 cups.

Nutty granola is nutritious and tasty eaten out of hand as a snack food. It can also be used as a dessert topping for baked apples, a fresh fruit cup, a *Yogurt Sundae* (see recipe), or sprinkled atop yogurt that has been swirled with honey or applesauce.

A LIST OF COMMON FOOD ADDITIVES

Additive	Source, Use, and Application	Safety
Acids: Acetic, Adipic, Citric, Sorbic	Found naturally in fruits and vegetables; also synthesized and used as a preservative and to add tartness to beverages, confections, desserts, cheeses, pickles, preserves.	On the FDA's (Food and Drug Administration's) GRAS ("generally recognized as safe") list. Other testing groups have reported no known danger.
Agar-Agar; Alginates	Obtained from seaweed; used like gelatin as a thickener and stabilizer for ice cream, yogurt, frostings.	GRAS No known danger.
Ascorbic Acid (Vitamin C)	Found naturally in citrus fruits, rose hips, etc.; also synthesized for use as antioxidant (preservative) and for nutritional fortification, in oily foods, cured meats, beverages.	No known danger, but excessive amounts taken as a presumed cold preventative may have harmful side effects.
Baking powder; Baking Soda (Sodium Bicarbonate)	Synthetic leavening agents, used in baked goods. Sodium bicarbonate is also used as an antacid.	GRAS No known danger in reasonable use.
Brominated Vegetable Oil	Synthetically treated oil, used as an emulsifier in citrus-flavored beverages, ice creams, baked goods.	Suspected as dangerous; poisonous residues may be stored in body tissues. On GRAS list awaiting FDA action but not banned from use.

BHA (Butylated Hydroxyanisole); BHT (Butylated Hydroxytoluene)	Synthetic antioxidants (preservatives) used in potato chips, salad oils, candies, chewing gum, dry cereals, cake mixes, dehydrated potato flakes.	BHT is a suspected carcinogen; both are allergenic. In continued use, pending further FDA study.
Caffeine	Found naturally in coffee, tea, kola nuts. Obtained largely through manufacture of caffeine-free coffee, and used to flavor colas and other soft drinks, and as a stimulant.	Causes nervousness, insomnia; hyperactivity in children; possibly birth defects. FDA study pending re levels in foods consumed by children.
Calcium Propionate	Synthetic fungicide (preservative) used to prevent mold and rope growth in commercial baked goods.	GRAS No known danger.
Carotene	Found naturally in carrots, egg yolk, butter, and is converted by body into vitamin A. Extracted for use as a coloring and a nutrient in butter, margarine, and other real and imitation dairy products.	No known danger except that vitamin A is stored in body and excessive amounts can produce harmful symptoms.
Carrageenan	Obtained from Irish moss; used as a thickener and stabilizer in chocolate products, whipped toppings, frozen desserts, infant formulas.	Removed from GRAS list, but still in use pending FDA study for suspected role in causing birth abnormalities; also inflammation of the colon, especially in infants.
Casein; Sodium Caseinate	Found naturally in cow's milk. Extracted for use as a thickener, texturizer, and whitener in ice cream and other frozen desserts, and in imitation dairy products.	GRAS No known danger.

Additive	Source, Use, and Application	Safety
Corn Syrup (Dextrose)	Found naturally as the sugar in corn. Converted for use as a flavoring and/or to prevent crystalization in confections, jellies, frozen desserts, baked goods, soft drinks, beers, bourbon whiskey, and wines, and in many nonsweet processed foods.	GRAS No known danger, except that it contributes to excessive sugar intake, and may cause allergic reaction in individuals sensitive to corn products.
Cream of Tartar (Tartaric Acid)	Found naturally in grapes as tartaric acid. Synthesized for use as the acid in some baking powders, and is used as a buffer in many sweet and artificially sweetened foods.	GRAS No known danger.
Dyes, Artificial	Among synthetic colorings and coal-tar derivatives are: Blue No. 1, Blue No. 2, Citrus Red No. 2, Green No. 3, Red No. 3, Red No. 40, Orange B, and Yellow No. 5. Used widely in soft drinks, gelatin desserts, ice cream, dry cereals, baked goods, confections. Citrus Red No. 2 is used to color orange skins; Red No. 3 to color cherries; Orange B to color frankfurters.	Despite "certified" ratings; as approved FD&C (Food, Drug, and Cosmetic) colors, some are under suspicion as carcinogenic to animals, some are allergens, and all appear to require further testing.
EDTA (Ethylene-diamine Tetraacetate)	Synthetic sequestrant (chelating agent) that traps metallic impurities to prevent rancidity and discoloration. Used in soft drinks, canned fish, margarine, mayonnaise, salad dressing.	No proven toxicity, but FDA study is pending re possible effects as skin irritant and/or allergen.
Flavorings, Artificial	Synthethic flavorings form largest category of additives, about 1,600, and are used largely in junk foods and other processed foods.	Many are potent compounds believed capable of causing hyperactivity in children. In some cases, very small amounts in pure concentrated form can cause convulsions and death.

Fumaric Acid	Found naturally in plants. Synthesized for use as a flavoring in gelatin desserts and confections, and also as a leavening agent, similar in action to tartaric acid, in baked goods.	GRAS No known danger.
Gelatin	Obtained from animal bones and other hard tissues. Used as a thickener in gelatin desserts, ices, ice cream, cheese spreads, chocolate-milk drinks.	No known danger, but should not be considered of high nutritional value, as it is a poor source of protein lacking certain essential amino acids.
Glycerides, Mono- and Diglycerides	Derived from fats and oils; used as emulsifying and defoaming agents to keep peanut butter, puddings, and topping mixtures from separating, and to keep bubbles from forming in fruit juices and other liquids; also to keep baked goods from drying out.	GRAS, but FDA study pending to determine possible link to birth abnormalities.
Glycerin (Glycerol)	Obtained from fats and oils; used as a humectant (moisturizer) to retain softness in marshmallows and other confections and in baked goods.	No known danger.
Gums: Acacia (Arabic), Carob Bean, Ghatti, Guar, Karaya, Tragacanth	Derived from plants and used as thickeners and stabilizers in puddings, frozen desserts, baked goods, confections, salad dressings, cheeses, milk shakes and other thickened beverages.	GRAS, but may cause allergic reactions, and some are scheduled to be reevaluated by FDA as possible links to birth abnormalities.
Heptyl Paraben (Heptyl-para-hydroxyben-zoate)	Synthetic preservative used in beer.	No proven danger, but interaction with alcohol, smoke, and proteins may be carcinogenic.

Additive	Source, Use, and Application	Safety
Hydrolyzed Vegetable Protein (HVP)	Derived from soybeans and other vegetables, and used as flavor enhancer in soups and gravies, and in baby and junior foods.	GRAS, but some studies recommend that levels used in young children's foods be studied for possible adverse effects.
Invert Sugar	A combination of glucose and fructose, both derived from fruits and other plants, and sweeter than sucrose. Used in candies where extra sweetness and moisture retention are required.	GRAS No known danger, but contributes to excessive intake of sugar which has potentially harmful effects.
Lactic Acid	Found naturally in sour milk, fruits, and molasses. Extracted for use as a flavoring and/or preservative in beverages, frozen and other desserts, confections, baked goods, preserves, pickles, olives, cheeses, and infant formulas.	No known danger, although concentration in infant feeding may be too high.
Lactose (Milk Sugar)	Sugar naturally found in milk. Less sweet than sucrose and used in infant formulas, whipped toppings, and other foods requiring mild sweetening.	No known danger.
Lecithin	Found naturally in plant and animal tissues, and a source of the nutrient choline. Extracted from eggs, soybeans, and corn for use as an emulsifier and antioxidant in margarine, chocolate, frozen desserts, baked goods, and dry cereals.	No known danger.

Additive	Description	Safety
Malic Acid	Found in fruits and other plants. Extracted or synthesized for use as a maturing agent in winemaking and to flavor many artificially sweetened foods.	No known danger.
Mannitol	Derived from seaweed and other plants for use as a mild sweetener in sugarless gum and as a dusting agent and texturizer in regular gums and candies.	Poorly absorbed by body and may have laxative or other gastrointestinal effects.
Modified Starch	Natural plant starch treated with chemicals, including soda lye, to increase digestibility. Used as thickener and texturizer in baby foods, soups, gravies, and other processed foods.	FDA reevaluation pending because chemical content may be harmful to young children.
MSG (Monosodium Glutamate)	Found naturally in seaweed, soybeans, and sugar beets. Extracted or synthesized for use as a flavor enhancer in numerous processed and precooked foods.	GRAS, but causes "Chinese Restaurant Syndrome." Further FDA study pending because of suspected links to reproductive and birth abnormalities and to infant brain damage.
Polysorbates	Synthetic emulsifiers, similar in function to lecithin and to mono- and diglycerides, used to keep mixtures from separating. Polysorbate 60 is found in frozen desserts, puddings, whipped toppings and other imitation dairy products, cake mixes, and confections.	No proven danger, but further FDA study pending.
Propyl Gallate	Synthetic antioxidant (preservative) used in oils, potato chips, meat products, and also as a freshness preserver in candies, chewing gum, gelatin desserts and other mixes.	GRAS, but amounts restricted pending further testing.

Additive	Source, Use, and Application	Safety
Quinine	Extracted from bark of the tropical cinchona tree and used in treatment of malaria. Also a flavoring agent in "bitter lemon" and "tonic water," some alcoholic beverages, and in various nonprescription medicines.	Causes allergic reactions in some individuals, and a high intake may be linked to birth defects.
Saccharin (Sodium Saccharin)	Synthetic noncaloric sweetener used in soft drinks, diet foods, and as a tabletop sugar substitute.	Removed from GRAS list in 1972. Causes bladder cancer in rats. Pending FDA action to ban it or make it a prescription drug, foods containing saccharin carry health-risk-warning labels.
Sodium Benzoate	Synthetic preservative used in acid foods like fruit juices, carbonated drinks, maraschino cherries, preserves, pickles.	GRAS, but may cause allergic reactions or intestinal disturbances in some individuals.
Sodium Bisulfite	Synthetic preservative, bleaching and antibrowning agent. Used in wine and beer, and in cut fruits that have been canned, frozen, or dried; also in fresh mushrooms.	GRAS, but FDA scheduled to reevaluate safe levels of use.
Sodium Nitrate, Sodium Nitrite	Synthetic preservatives that also provide flavoring and fix the red color in cured meats and fish. Nitrates are used in long-cured country-style hams and dried sausages, while the more widely used nitrites are found in frankfurters, bacon, ham, corned beef, bologna and other luncheon meats, and smoked fish.	Converted in the human body into cancer-causing nitrosamines. Not banned, pending FDA or USDA action.

[178]

Name	Description	Status
Sorbitan Monostearate	Synthetic emulsifier used to prevent oil and water separation in chocolate, frostings, cakes, whipped toppings, frozen desserts, and nondairy coffee creamers.	No known danger.
Sorbitol	Found in berries and other fruits. Extracted or synthesized for use as a mild sweetener, thickener, and humectant (moisturizer) in chewing gum, candy, shredded coconut, dietetic drinks and foods.	GRAS No known danger, but excessive amounts may cause intestinal disturbances. May be safe for diabetics due to slow absorption by body, but levels of use require further testing.
Sulfur Dioxide	Gas from burning of sulfur. Used as a bleach and preservative for dried and preserved fruits, corn syrup, wines.	GRAS, but gas has poisonous properties as an inhalant. Further FDA study pending.
Tannic Acid	Obtained from coffee, tea, and plant barks. Used as a flavoring in caramel, maple, and nut extracts for alcoholic and nonalcoholic beverages, baked goods, and ice cream, and as a clarifying agent in wine- and beer-making.	GRAS, but may cause stomach distress in some individuals.
Vanillin	Synthetic vanilla flavoring, used in baked goods, chocolate, candy, ice cream, puddings, beverages.	GRAS No known danger.

BIBLIOGRAPHY

Boorstin, Daniel J. *The Americans: The Democratic Experience.* N.Y.: Random House, 1973.

DeVore, Sally and White, Thelma. *The Appetites of Man.* N.Y.: Anchor/ Doubleday, 1978.

Doyle, Rodger P. and Redding, James L. *The Complete Food Handbook.* N.Y.: Grove Press, 1978.

Doyle, Rodger. *The Vegetarian Handbook.* N.Y.: Crown, 1979.

Furnas, J. C. *Great Times.* N.Y.: Putnam, 1974.

Goldbeck, Nikki and David. *The Supermarket Handbook.* N.Y.: Harper & Row, 1973.

Hess, John L. and Karen. *The Taste of America.* N.Y.: Grossman/Viking, 1976.

Hewitt, Jean. *The New York Times Natural Foods Cookbook.* N.Y.: Avon, 1972.

Hightower, Jim. *Eat Your Heart Out: Food Profiteering in America.* N.Y.: Crown, 1975.

Hunter, Beatrice Trum. *Consumer Beware: Your Food and What's Been Done to It.* N.Y.: Simon & Schuster, 1971.

———. *The Great Nutrition Robbery.* N.Y.: Scribner's, 1978.

Jacobson, Michael. *Eater's Digest: The Consumer's Factbook of Food Additives.* N.Y.: Anchor/Doubleday, 1976.

Keats, John. *What Ever Happened to Mom's Apple Pie?* Boston: Houghton Mifflin, 1976.

Lasky, Michael. *The Complete Junk Food Book.* N.Y.: McGraw-Hill, 1977.

Margolius, Sidney. *The Great American Food Hoax.* N.Y.: Walker, 1971.

McClure, Jon A. *Meat Eaters Are Threatened.* N.Y.: Pyramid, 1973.

Robbins, William. *The American Food Scandal.* N.Y.: Morrow, 1974.

Schrank, Jeffrey. *Snap, Crackle, and Popular Taste: The Illusion of Free Choice in America.* N.Y.: Dell, 1977.

Stare, Frederick J. and McWilliams, Margaret. *Living Nutrition.* N.Y.: John Wiley & Sons, 2d ed., 1977.

Trager, James. *The Bellybook.* N.Y.: Grossman, 1972.

Verrett, Jacqueline and Carper, Jean. *Eating May Be Hazardous to Your Health.* N.Y.: Simon & Schuster, 1974.

Wellford, Harrison. *Sowing the Wind.* N.Y.: Grossman, 1972.

Winter, Ruth. *A Consumer's Dictionary of Food Additives.* N.Y.: Crown, 1978.

INDEX